The Seasons at Walden Inn

The Seasons at Walden Inn

Signature Recipes

From an Elegant Country Inn

MATTHEW O'NEILL

Guild Press of Indiana
Carmel, Indiana

GUILD PRESS OF INDIANA, INC.
435 Gradle Drive
Carmel, IN 46032

Library of Congress
Catalog Card Number
97-73768

ISBN 1-57860-004-9

Printed in the United States of America

Cover photograph by Rita Harold
Cover design by Steven D. Armour
Text design by Sheila G. Samson

Within this book: Watercolor of the Walden Inn by Bruce Dean Johnson. Photographs of leek preparation, the gingerbread house, and apple swan by Jack Westhead. Remaining photographs by Lesle McGuire Tomlin of McGuire Photography.

Contents

This work is dedicated to the memory of
Karen Jansen O'Neill

Acknowledgments

I am grateful for the positive influence of many people on the creation of this cookbook. They fall into two groups:

First, there are those who guided the Walden Inn itself from concept to reality. Without them there would be no Walden Inn and thus no inspiration for the book. These include Don Daseke, Nancy Bisgair, Sue Ansul, Larry Taylor, and Bob and Gwen Bottoms. They are the ones who conceived of the Inn, nurtured it into being, and entrusted it—for better or for worse—into my stewardship.

Secondly, there are those who enthusiastically tested, tasted, tweaked, critiqued, sniffed, substituted, and squashed various ingredients and recipes. I must not forget either those who rummaged through my prose with such gusto, ferreting out mistakes in punctuation and exposing my alarmingly casual use of colons, semicolons, commas, and periods. High on this list is my publisher, Nancy Baxter, who believed in me; and Sheila Samson, my editor and book designer, for her meticulous attention to detail and for letting me play with her cats. Thanks also to my friends Theresa Hendrixon, Rachael Royster, Craig Owens, Molly Murray, Gil Duran, Janice Brothers, and Chelsea Smock for proofreading, advice, and support.

I'm grateful to Jodie Ensley, brilliant cutting-edge chef and Culinary Institute of America (CIA) alumnus, for testing and for culling the too-corny recipes from the book. And to Jeff Danielson, owner of the Runcible Spoon coffee shop in Bloomington, Indiana, where I wrote most of the book on my laptop computer while I hogged his tables and drank the best coffee in the state.

To my son, Matt Jr. — we will always be a team. Thanks to Brooke Sanderson Ridell, who, on a drowsy summer evening several years ago, talked me into taking that creative writing workshop. And to Kate Bostwick, Bridget Harvey, and Kay Weaver for ingredient substitutions, testing, and enhancement of the bread recipes.

Thanks also to Walter Shreyer of the Culinary Institute of America; Wolfgang Puck of Spago; and Pier Roland and the late Hector Fabron of the Russell Hotel in Dublin, Ireland, for being inspirational mile markers along the way.

Finally, thanks to my father, the late Mattie O'Neill. Even though he is gone, his hand is still on my shoulder. It emboldens me now as it did then, when, at the age of fifteen, I first walked through the back door of a hotel kitchen, into a clattering chorus of pots and pans to present myself for work to the chef and his cast of cooks.

Matthew O'Neill
Greencastle, Indiana
June 1999

Introduction

This book was written in reference to a particular Inn, but it is really a celebration of special places and kitchens everywhere—places that respond to the ever-turning carousel of the months, capturing the miracle of the changing seasons in the meshes of their nets to give them culinary expression.

Seasons at Walden

The seasons, like a lilting carousel of
ponies winding 'round the Walden Inn,
are turning through life's carnival
of changelessness and change.

Spring is wobbly with hope, its
ride a bit uneven, like someone
shook out a bag of butterflies
found sleeping somewhere
deep in Winter's wrinkled husk.

Summer's pony's fast asleep,
dreaming it's a covered bridge,
a peephole to eternity, happy
to be a backwater, contented
and silent in the knowledge
that sometimes the best times
are had in places half forgotten.

Autumn is a hunter for the lovelorn,
who has found the secret
tapestry of some lost beloved's
soul, and stretched it across the
countryside to break another heart.

And now comes old, unwanted
Winter once more,
that wandering tinker's donkey,
standing in the Inn's half-open
door, firelight reflecting on
his snowflake-covered lashes,
mildly watching while we look
to find that half-remembered name
in the pages of the reservation book.

Walden's innkeeper, Matthew O'Neill

The dining room of Walden Inn of Greencastle.

Winter

January

brings New Year's Day, and the windows of the Inn are winking like a new-born's eyes from a snow-swaddled winter blanket. The last guest to toast in the new and tip a paper hat to the memory of the old has straggled off to bed, leaving behind streamers and plastic bugles washed up on January's frosty shore.

January is a time for foods of comfort and warmth, using recipes and techniques tested by generations of practice, sometimes giving them a creative twist by using unique combinations. At the Inn we customarily serve onion and garlic soup and roasted chicken with seared artichokes, mushrooms, and potatoes.

My personal favorite for this time of year is a coq au vin using free range chicken. This French classic I learned as an apprentice from my first chef-mentor, Jacky Needham, a kind Dubliner with a dough-boy profile, an impish face, and a persistent but polite sounding smoker's cough.

With mastery and meticulous attention to detail and method, the recipe would unfold before my fifteen-year-old eyes as the classic dish came to life in Jacky's skillful hands. "Did you understand that now, son?" he would ask in his quiet paternal voice after each step. Jacky and that magnificent old Georgian hotel where he performed his art are no longer around, but he is with me in spirit every time I prepare this dish. "That's the way, son," I hear him say in his soft Dublin accent. "Don't be tempted to take shortcuts—there's a good reason for every step."

Chicken with Spinach and Figs

Serves 4

4	5-ounce boneless, skinless chicken breasts
2	tablespoons vegetable oil
4	medium garlic cloves, peeled and minced
	Salt and pepper
6	shallots, peeled and finely chopped
¼	cup chardonnay
3	cups loosely packed torn fresh spinach
12	dried figs, coarsely chopped
1	tablespoon coarsely chopped basil
½	teaspoon chopped fresh chives
¼	teaspoon chopped fresh sage
¼	teaspoon chopped fresh rosemary
¼	teaspoon chopped fresh thyme
½	teaspoon ground nutmeg
1 ½	cups chicken broth
	Arugula

Preheat the oven to 375°.

Rub the chicken breasts with oil, garlic, and salt and pepper to taste. Sauté the chicken breasts in an oven-proof skillet over high heat, 6 minutes per side. Remove chicken to a warm platter and set aside.

Keeping the skillet over high heat, add the chopped shallot and sauté, stirring, for 1 minute. Add the chardonnay and cook for 1 minute. Add the spinach and figs and continue cooking, stirring, for 1 more minute.

Return the chicken to the skillet. Pour the broth over all and add the basil, chives, rosemary, and thyme. Place skillet in the oven and bake for 10 minutes.

To serve, arrange the chicken on a bed of the spinach. Spoon the figs over the chicken with some of the pan juices, and garnish with a sprig of arugula.

Cranberry Orange Walnut Bread

Makes 3 loaves

6	cups all-purpose flour
½	teaspoon salt
1	cup instant vanilla pudding mix
1	tablespoon plus 1 teaspoon baking powder
2	cups sugar
1	cup (2 sticks) butter, softened
3	cups orange juice
1	tablespoon grated orange peel
5	eggs
1 ½	cups sweetened dried cranberries
1	cup coarsely chopped walnuts

Grease and flour three 8 x 4-inch loaf pans. Preheat oven to 350°.

Sift together the flour, salt, pudding mix, and baking powder in a large bowl.

With a mixer, beat the sugar and butter together until light and fluffy. In another bowl, beat together the orange juice, orange peel, and eggs.

Alternately add the dry ingredients and the orange juice mixture to the creamed butter and sugar, stirring just enough to blend the ingredients. Do not overmix.

Toss the walnuts in just enough flour to lightly coat them. (This will keep them from sinking to the bottom of the pans during baking.) Gently fold the walnuts and cranberries into the batter.

Scoop the batter into the prepared loaf pans and bake for 35–40 minutes or until done. Place on a wire rack and allow to cool in pans for 15 minutes. Remove the loaves from the pans and finish cooling on the wire rack.

Double Chocolate Fillo Pockets

6   ounces of white chocolate

7   ounces of semisweet chocolate

½   cup sugar

8   sheets of fillo dough

½   cup (1 stick) unsalted butter, melted

Grate or grind 3 ounces of the semisweet and 3 ounces of the white chocolate and mix with the ½ cup sugar.

Cut the remaining 4 ounces of the semisweet chocolate into half-ounce pieces.

Cut the fillo sheets lengthwise into 4 equal portions (about 3 ¼ inches wide). Take one sheet of fillo and brush with some melted butter and sprinkle with some of the sugar mixture. Add three more sheets, brushing with butter and sprinkling with the sugar mixture on each. You now have a stack of 4 strips.

Starting at the one end of the stack, place a half-ounce piece of the semisweet chocolate about 2 inches from the end. Fold the fillo flag-style over the chocolate to form a triangle. Continue folding until the pastry is all wrapped, and place seam-side down on a baking sheet. Repeat the process with the remaining fillo sheets. Bake in a preheated 350° oven until golden brown, about 10 minutes.

Chop the remaining 3 ounces of white chocolate. Place the chocolate in the top of a double boiler and heat over simmering water just until melted. Drizzle the melted chocolate with a fork over the triangles. Serve warm.

These fillo pockets are best served the day they are made, although they can be reheated.

Fennel and Bacon Patties

Serves 8

4   fennel bulbs, peeled and cubed
½   cup (1 stick) unsalted butter or margarine
1   cup plus 2 tablespoons sour cream
2   tablespoons chopped, cooked bacon
2   tablespoons minced fresh ginger
¼   cup all-purpose flour
     Salt and pepper
¼   cup corn meal for dusting
2   tablespoons olive oil

Cover the fennel in water and bring to a boil. When it is tender, drain and dry.

Mash the fennel with the butter. Add the sour cream, bacon, ginger, flour, and salt and pepper to taste. Cover and refrigerate for about one hour.

Shape mixture into patties, 2 ½ inches in diameter and ¼- to ½-inch thick. Dust in cornmeal and sauté in olive oil over medium heat for about 6 minutes each side, until golden.

Skillet-Seared New York Strip Steaks and Mushrooms

Serves 4

4   10-ounce New York strip steaks
2   tablespoons vegetable oil
3   teaspoons minced garlic
    Salt and pepper
2   tablespoons minced shallots
1 ½ cups sliced mushrooms
½   cup chardonnay
¼   cup soy sauce
2   teaspoons Dijon mustard
1   teaspoon beef base

Rub the steaks with the oil and garlic and season with salt and pepper.

Preheat a large heavy skillet over high heat. Add the steaks and sear on both sides, about 6 minutes per side for rare, 7 minutes for medium-rare, and 8 minutes for medium. (The steaks should have a nice brown, slightly crispy crust.) Transfer the steaks to a warm platter and place in a warm oven while preparing the sauce.

In the same skillet the steaks were cooked in, sauté the shallots on high heat until they are transluscent. Add the mushrooms and cook for 2 minutes more.

Add the chardonnay, soy sauce, mustard, and beef base. Continue cooking for 5 more minutes. Spoon the sauce over the steaks and serve.

Herbed Mini-Biscuits
with Andouille Sausage and Wild Mushrooms

The tiny biscuit cutters for these hors d'oeuvres can be found in specialty cooking shops or restaurant supply stores.

Serves 8

Mini-biscuits

2	cups cake flour
1/2	teaspoon salt
3 1/4	teaspoons baking powder
1	tablespoon fresh chopped tarragon
2	teaspoons fresh chopped dill
1	teaspoon fresh chopped rosemary
1/2	teaspoon fresh chopped sage
1/2	teaspoon fresh chopped thyme
1/2	teaspoon saffron
5	tablespoons lard or vegetable shortening
1	cup milk

Gravy

1/2	cup finely diced andouille sausage
1/2	cup sliced assorted wild mushrooms
2	tablespoons (1/4 stick) unsalted butter
1	tablespoon flour
1 1/2	tablespoons bourbon
1	cup chicken broth

FOR THE MINI-BISCUITS: Sift the cake flour, salt, and baking powder together into a large bowl. Add the herbs. With a pastry blender or fingers, work the lard or shortening into the flour mixture just until it resembles very coarse meal. Take care not to overblend.

Add the milk and mix until dough forms a soft ball. Turn the dough onto a lightly floured surface and knead gently until it is smooth. Flatten the dough to a circle slightly less than 1/2 inch thick. Cut dough into 3/4- to 1-inch rounds with a sharp edged cookie cutter. Bake at 350° for 5–7 minutes or until light brown.

FOR THE GRAVY: Sauté the sausage and the wild mushrooms over medium heat. Add the butter.

When butter is melted, add the flour and stir well. Add the bourbon and chicken broth and continue cooking, stirring constantly, until thick.

Serve the mini-biscuits on a platter with the gravy in a tureen or chafing dish on the side, and allow guests to help themselves.

Oatmeal and Nut Encrusted Red Snapper with Red Pepper and Tomatillo Salsa

Serves 4

4	6-ounce red snapper filets
2	whole red peppers, roasted, seeded, and peeled
4	tomatillos, husked
¼	cup balsamic vinegar
1	tablespoon chopped fresh cilantro
1	cup rolled oats
1	cup walnuts
1	whole egg (or 2 egg whites)
2	tablespoons flour
2	tablespoons Dijon mustard
½	cup milk
2	tablespoons vegetable oil

In a blender or food processor, purée the red peppers and tomatillos until smooth. Transfer to a bowl and add the balsamic vinegar and cilantro.

Toast the walnuts and crush by pulsing once or twice in a food processor (do not overprocess); combine with the oatmeal. Combine the eggs, flour, mustard, and milk to form a batter. Dip the fish filets in the batter and lightly coat with the oatmeal-walnut mixture. Heat oil in an oven-proof skillet over medium heat and sauté fish 6 minutes per side, until golden brown. Place in a preheated 375° oven and bake for 8 minutes.

Serve the snapper on a pool of the salsa.

Walden Inn Black Bean Soup

Serves 4

1 ½ cups dried black beans
2–3 cups (approximately) chicken or vegetable broth or water
1   tablespoon vegetable oil
¾   cup mushrooms, sliced
½   cup scallions
¾   cup chopped fresh tomatoes
½   cup chopped sun-dried tomatoes
     Salt and pepper
1   tablespoon sherry (optional)
     Sour cream

Rinse the black beans and soak overnight in a medium saucepan. Drain the beans and add the broth or water (the beans should be covered by about 4 inches of liquid). Bring to a boil. Reduce heat to simmer and cook for about 2 hours or until beans are done, stirring occasionally. (Do not undercook the beans. When they are done, they will burst and have a tender, pasty consistency.) Add more liquid as needed while cooking to keep the beans froom scorching.

Heat the oil in a small saucepan or skillet and sauté the sliced mushrooms. Remove from heat, and add the scallions and the tomatoes. Stir the mushrooms, tomatoes, and scallions into the bean soup and season with salt and pepper to taste.

Stir in sherry just before serving. Ladle soup into bowls, garnish with dollops of sour cream and serve.

Note: If you don't have time to cook the beans, one 15-ounce can of black beans may be substituted. Add ½ to ¾ cup of broth, and proceed as above with the rest of the directions.

Basic Black Beans

Several recipes in this book, besides the Walden Inn Black Bean Soup, call for black beans. Following are the basic steps for preparing black beans.

Rinse one cup of dried black beans. Place in a medium-size pan and cover with water and soak overnight.

Drain the soaking water from the beans and add broth or water to cover by about 4 inches. Bring to a boil, reduce heat to simmer, and cook beans for about 2 hours, stirring occasionally. Add liquid as needed during cooking so the beans will not scorch.

When the beans are done, they will burst and have a tender, pasty consistency.

Onion Steak Sauce

3	medium onions
3	tablespoons vegetable oil
2	cups tomato sauce
3	tablespoons Worcestershire sauce
2	tablespoons vinegar
4	tablespoons molasses
4	tablespoons coarse-grained Dijon mustard
2	garlic cloves, minced
	Juice of half a lemon
	Salt and pepper to taste

Peel and thinly slice the onions into a mixing bowl. Add the vegetable oil and stir until onions are coated. Spread the onions on a baking tray and roast in a preheated 375° oven for 15 minutes.

Put the roasted onions in a heavy saucepan and add the remaining ingredients. Stirring constantly, cook over moderate heat for 15 minutes until mixture becomes slightly carmelized. Delicious served with New York strip steaks, t-bones, and filet mignons.

Wild Rice, Pecan, and Tomato Pancakes

Makes 12 pancakes

¼ cup chopped pecans
½ cup all-purpose flour
½ teaspoon baking powder
½ teaspoon baking soda
  Salt and pepper
½ cup milk
1 large egg, beaten
⅔ cup cooked wild rice (see page 88)
2 tablespoons chopped shallots
¼ cup chopped tomatoes
2 tablespoons olive oil

Spread pecans on a baking sheet and toast in a 375° oven for 5 minutes. Set aside.

Combine the flour, baking powder, and baking soda in a bowl. Add salt and pepper to taste. In another bowl blend the egg and milk. Add the dry ingredients. Add the cooked wild rice, shallots, tomatoes, and pecans.

Heat the olive oil in a skillet over medium-high heat. Drop the pancake mixture by spoonfuls into the hot oil and cook for about 5 minutes each side, or until the edges are crispy.

February

is faith in things unseen, Spring waiting in the womb of an aging Winter. Its gift to us is the pleasure of anticipation, the heart and soul of romance. I cannot imagine Valentine's Day existing in any other month.

Our cooking at the Inn, like the character of February, takes on a distinct duality. On the one hand we concoct desserts like homemade chocolate truffles and heart-shaped baked Alaskas. On the other, we introduce lighter dishes in guilty anticipation of the waist-conscious weather on the way. In like manner, we enjoy winter things like snow glowing softly in lamplight, while we dream of the inexorable slow warming of the senses that will steal across the heart of the world in the coming months.

Chocolate Mascarpone Raspberry Flan

Serves 8–10

Flan shell

1 ¼   cups all-purpose flour

1   tablespoon sugar

¼   teaspoon salt

½   cup (1 stick butter) butter, well chilled and cut in small pieces

2 ½   tablespoons very cold water

Filling

½   cup heavy cream

2   ounces bittersweet chocolate, chopped in small pieces

1   cup mascarpone cheese

4   tablespoons sugar

2   teaspoons raspberry liqueur

1   pint fresh raspberries

FOR FLAN SHELL: Combine the flour, sugar, salt, and butter in a bowl. With a pastry blender or your fingers, blend just until the mixture resembles coarse meal. Add the water a bit at a time and blend gently, just until the dough forms a soft mass. Wrap the dough in plastic wrap and refrigerate for 30 minutes.

On a lightly floured surface, roll the dough into a circle about 11 inches in diameter and about ⅛ inch thick. Lightly dust the bottom of a 9-inch spring-form pan with flour. Gently press the dough into the pan, forming a 1-inch rim all around. Line the shell with foil and place pie weights on the foil. Bake the shell in a preheated 375° oven for 15 minutes, or until golden. Remove from the oven and carefully remove the weights and the foil.

FOR FILLING: Scald the cream in a saucepan over medium heat. Add the chocolate and immediately remove from heat. Let stand until the chocolate is melted, about 3 minutes. Stir until smooth.

In a bowl, whisk the mascarpone until fluffy. Whisk in the sugar, liqueur, and chocolate-cream mixture. Refrigerate for 15 minutes, until firm. Fill the flan shell with the chocolate-cheese mixture and arrange the raspberries in concentric circles around the top.

Eggplant and Walnut Pancakes

½   cup chopped walnuts
1   medium eggplant
3   tablespoons chopped scallions
3   tablespoons olive oil
1   large egg, beaten
1   tablespoon all-purpose flour
2   tablespoons sour cream
    Salt and pepper

Spread the walnuts on a baking sheet and bake in a 375° oven for 5 minutes. Set aside.

Peel and dice the eggplant into ¼-inch cubes. Sauté the eggplant, scallions, and toasted walnuts in 1 tablespoon of olive oil over medium heat for about 8 minutes.

Blend the egg and the flour. Add the sour cream and eggplant mixture. Season with salt and pepper to taste.

Wipe the sauté skillet clean and add 2 tablespoons olive oil. Preheat over medium heat and spoon pancake mixture in. Brown on both sides, about 6 minutes per side.

Oriental Shrimp and Vegetable Rolls

You can find the rice "paper" wrappers for this dish in Oriental food stores. They are actually edible, crêpe-like wrappers that are almost transluscent, allowing you to see the colorful contents.

Serves 4

16   medium-sized shrimp, peeled and deveined
1   tablespoon peanut oil
⅓   cup julienned celery (sliced into small slender sticks, approximately 2 inches long)
⅓   cup julienned carrots
⅓   cup julienned leek
½   teaspoon soy sauce
2   tablespoons medium dry sherry
1   teaspoon hoisin sauce
1   teaspoon hazelnut oil
1   teaspoon chopped and crushed ginger
1   level tablespoon sesame seeds
4   sheets edible rice paper

Preheat a skillet or saucepan on high heat and add the peanut oil. Sauté the shrimp in the peanut oil until they turn pink and opaque, about 10 minutes. Add the vegetables and sauté another 6 minutes. (Do not overcook; the vegetables should be *al dente*—slightly firm to the bite.)

Add the soy sauce, sherry, hazelnut oil, hoisin, ginger, and sesame seeds.

Soften the rice paper by soaking in a pan of warm water for about 15 seconds, or just until it becomes pliable. Fold the shrimp and vegetables in the rice papers like a crêpe and serve.

Medallions of Beef with Brandy and Peppercorn Sauce

This is a Walden Inn classic.

Serves 4

1	2-pound beef tenderloin
1 ½	teaspoons minced garlic
	Salt and pepper
2	tablespoons vegetable oil
1	tablespoon soft green Madagascar peppercorns
2	tablespoons cognac
¾	cup heavy cream
1	teaspoon beef base or ½ bouillon cube
1	tablespoon chopped fresh parsley

Cut the tenderloin across the grain to form twelve ½-inch-thick slices, or medallions. (Have the meat cutter do this, if you wish.)

Season the medallions with the garlic and salt and pepper. Heat oil in a large, heavy skillet over high heat. Add the medallions and sear on both sides.

Without reducing the heat, add the green peppercorns, cognac, cream, and base or bouillon. Shake the pan gently during cooking, and continue cooking until liquid is reduced to half the volume. Move the medallions occasionally with a fork during the cooking. Add the chopped parsley and remove from heat.

Spoon a pool of sauce on the bottoms of 4 plates and arrange 3 medallions on each.

Pecan and Herb Encrusted Halibut

Serves 4

4	5-ounce halibut filets
¼	cup fresh chopped basil
¼	cup chopped fresh cilantro
¼	cup chopped fresh tarragon
2	cups pecans
3	tablespoons Dijon mustard
⅓	cup milk
2	tablespoons olive oil

Preheat oven to 350°.

Combine the basil, tarragon, and cilantro. Coarsely chop or crush the pecans and add to the herbs.

Combine the milk and the mustard. Dip the halibut in the milk and the mustard and coat with the pecan-herb mix.

Heat the oil in an oven-proof skillet and sauté the fish over medium-high heat 6 minutes. Transfer the pan to the oven and bake for 8–10 minutes.

This is excellent served on a pool of Chef Vernon's Roasted Red Pepper Remoulade (page 105).

Roulade of Crab Meat and Smoked Salmon

Serves 4

6	ounces crab meat
2	ounces cream cheese, softened
8	slices smoked salmon
2	tablespoons prepared cocktail sauce
12	leaves Bibb lettuce

Finely chop the crab meat and mix well with the cream cheese.

Spread the cocktail sauce thinly on the smoked salmon, and spread the crab meat and cream cheese mixture over the cocktail sauce. Roll salmon slices into pinwheel shapes and serve on the leaves of Bibb lettuce.

Salmon Poached in Lettuce with Blackberry Hollandaise

Serves 4

4	6-ounce salmon filets
1	teaspoon minced garlic
	Salt and pepper
4	large leaves of leaf or romaine lettuce
1	quart water or fish stock
4	egg yolks
1	cup (2 sticks) butter
	Juice of 1 large lemon
1	cup fresh blackberries

Soak the lettuce leaves in warm water until they become limp and pliable.

Season the salmon filets with garlic and salt and pepper and wrap with the lettuce leaves.

In a large pan, bring the water or fish stock just to a boil and reduce heat to simmer. Carefully place the wrapped fish in the liquid and poach for 20 minutes.

Meanwhile, melt butter in a saucepan, skimming the foam off the top as it forms.

For the hollandaise, combine the egg yolks with the lemon juice in a stainless steel bowl. Place the bowl in a larger bowl with very hot water and whisk the yolk mixture until it is smooth and pale yellow. (You should be able to trace a ribbon along the bottom of the bowl.)

Remove yolk mixture from the water bath. Whisking constantly, slowly add the melted butter. Continue to whisk until the mixture is smooth.

In a small saucepan, bring 1 cup of water to a simmer and poach the blackberries for 5 minutes; drain. Reserve half the berries and mash the rest. Add the mashed blackberries to the hollandaise.

To serve, spread the blackberry hollandaise on the bottom of a plate and place the lettuce-wrapped salmon on top. Garnish with the whole berries.

Note: For a lighter and simpler alternative, you can substitute Champagne and Vanilla Yogurt Sauce (page 105) in place of the hollandaise.

Shrimp and Clam Ragout in Angel Hair Pasta Nest

Serves 4

12   clams
2   tablespoons olive oil
20   medium-sized raw shrimp, peeled and deveined
2   medium yellow summer squash, sliced
2   red peppers roasted, peeled, seeded, and sliced (page 52)
½   cup chopped scallions
1   level tablespoon chopped sun-dried tomatoes
2   fresh tomatoes, chopped
¾   cup sliced mushrooms
1   tablespoon pesto
¼   cup chardonnay
2   tablespoons grated Parmesan cheese
        Angel hair pasta (for 4 servings)

Boil or steam the clams until shells open.

Sauté shrimp lightly in the olive oil over medium-high heat for 5 minutes. Add the next 7 ingredients and continue cooking 5 more minutes.

Add the chardonnay and continue to cook until liquid is reduced by half.

Bring 1 ½ quarts of water to a rolling boil. Add angel hair pasta and cook until *al dente* (about 3 minutes) or according to package directions.

Drain the pasta. Arrange in a nest and serve with the ragout. Sprinkle with Parmesan cheese and serve.

Sweet Chocolate Cookie Crust Tart with Hazelnuts

Serves 6

1   cup broken-up Oreo cookies
½   cup (1 stick) butter
4 ½   cups hazelnuts
3   ounces unsweetened chocolate, chopped
6   tablespoons (¾ stick) unsalted butter

3	large eggs
⅛	teaspoon salt
½	cup granulated sugar
1	tablespoon maple syrup
2	tablespoons heavy cream
½	teaspoon vanilla extract
2	teaspoons brandy
½	cup semisweet chocolate chips
2	teaspoons ground cinnamon
1	teaspoon fivespice
1	teaspoon ground ginger
¼	cup sugar
2	cups whipped cream

Blend the cookies and ½ cup of butter in a food processor. Pulse until the mixture sticks together, adding more butter if needed, a little at a time. Press into the bottom of a 9-inch tart part.

Spread the hazlenuts on a baking sheet and toast in a 375° oven for 5 minutes and set aside. Reduce the oven heat to 325°.

Place the chocolate and butter together in the top of a double boiler and heat over simmering water, just until the chocolate begins to melt. (Take care that no water or steam gets into the chocolate mixture itself.) Remove from heat, and whisk until smooth.

In a mixing bowl, whisk together the eggs, salt, and sugar. Add the maple syrup and then the cream, vanilla extract, and brandy. Whisk until smooth and stir in the melted chocolate mixture.

Sprinkle the chocolate chips on the cookie crust. Pour the melted chocolate mixture over the chocolate chips.

Bake the tart 20–25 minutes until almost completely set. Chop the toasted hazelnuts and combine with ¼ cup sugar and spices. Serve the tart warm with a dollop of the whipped cream and a sprinkling of the hazelnut mixture on top. Serve extra whipped cream on the side.

Warm Spinach Salad with Mandarin Oranges

Serves 4

¼ cup olive oil
½ cup balsamic vinegar
½ cup fresh chopped tomato
1 tablespoon chopped sun-dried tomato
1 tablespoon Dijon mustard
5 cups loosely packed torn fresh spinach
¾ cup mandarin orange segments
½ cup Chinese noodles

Combine the olive oil, balsamic vinegar, fresh and dried tomatoes, and Dijon mustard and warm in a sauce pan. Toss with the spinach leaves in a bowl. Garnish with the mandarin oranges and the Chinese noodles and serve accompanied with Pesto, Goat Cheese, and Tomato Croutons (page 66).

March

brings to mind Ireland and St. Patrick's day. It is the bridge between the last protestations of a dying Winter and a Spring spilling out on wobbly Kelly green legs.

In the kitchen of the Walden, we pay homage to this heritage by preparing dishes I learned in the Dublin hotel where I received my training. It was an old Georgian building that presided in ancient elegance over the corners of Camden Street and St. Stephen's Green. The Hotel Russell held in its graceful bosom the secrets of my native city, and the peculiar dignity of Dublin's poverty crossed with its aristocratic Anglo-Irish heritage.

Its kitchens, located below street level, bristled with activity as an extremely disciplined brigade of chefs and apprentices prepared for lunch or dinner.

As a young apprentice, I was as attached to that building as I am to this one now. The kitchen of that old hotel was a heart whose pulse was the pursuit of culinary excellence. And like a classic Irish mead, it was distilled with the essence of the city's passing decades, mellowing and deepening with the honeyed passage of time.

Shrimp and Veal Dublin Bay

Serves 4

This recipe was cobbled together at a lake shore restaurant called the Waterfront. The evening view of the sunset on the water from the kitchen window would make me homesick for the ancient, legend-laced shoreline of Ireland.

12	ounces veal loin
	Salt and pepper
¼	cup all-purpose flour
¼	cup (½ stick) butter or margarine
	Juice of ¼ fresh lemon
12	medium-sized shrimp, peeled and deveined
1	red pepper, roasted, peeled, and seeded (page 52)
2	tablespoons cognac
2	tablespoons soft green peppercorns
1	teaspoon beef base, or 1 beef bouillon cube
¾	cup heavy cream or evaporated skim milk

Cut the veal into 8 slices (two 1 ½-ounce slices per serving). Season the veal with salt and pepper to taste, and lightly dust with flour.

Preheat a skillet over medium-high heat. Add the butter and when it sizzles add the lemon juice. Add the veal slices and cook on one side for 5 minutes; turn and add the shrimp and cook for 5 minutes longer.

Dice the red pepper and add to the veal and shrimp. Add the cognac, peppercorns, and the beef base or bouillon. Continue cooking until the shrimp and veal are coated with the mixture, about 5 minutes. Add the cream and season with salt and pepper to taste.

Arrange the veal in the center of the plate, place the shrimp on top, and drizzle the remaining sauce around the edge of the plate.

Irish Brown Soda Bread

Makes one large round loaf

1   cup plus 2 tablespoons all-purpose flour
4   cups whole wheat flour
⅓   cup toasted wheat germ
1 ½   teaspoons baking powder
1 ½   teaspoons baking soda
1 ½   teaspoons salt
1   tablespoon sugar
2 ⅓ cups buttermilk

Combine all of the dry ingredients. Add just enough of the buttermilk to form a slightly moist dough. Turn the dough out onto a lightly floured surface and knead until smooth, about 1 minute.

Shape the dough into an 8-inch round and place on a lightly greased baking sheet. With a sharp paring knife, cut crisscross lines across the top of the loaf, about ¼-inch deep.

Place the loaf in a preheated 400° oven and bake about 50 minutes, or until bread sounds hollow when tapped on the bottom. Wrap the loaf in a clean towel and set on a wire rack. Cool thoroughly before slicing.

Atlantic Salmon Galway Bay with Colcannon

Serves 4

Colcannon

4	large Idaho potatoes
1	whole leek, cleaned
1	scallion
¾	cup cooked spinach
1	cup (2 sticks) butter or margarine
1 ½	cups cream
	Salt and pepper

Salmon

¾	cup (1 ½ sticks) butter or margarine, softened
	Juice of half a lemon
	Salt and pepper
1 ½	pounds Atlantic salmon filet, cut into 4 portions
¾	cup chardonnay
2	scallions, chopped
12	large mushrooms, sliced

FOR COLCANNON: Peel the potatoes and cut them into quarters. In a saucepan, cover the potatoes with water and bring to a boil. Cook until they are soft in the center. (Do not allow the potatoes to cool before mashing and do not overmash or they will taste gummy.)

Mince the leek, scallion, and spinach. Add to the mashed potatoes along with the butter and cream. Add salt and pepper to taste.

FOR SALMON: Preheat oven to 350°. Coat a large baking dish with the butter or margarine. Add the lemon juice and sprinkle with salt and pepper to taste.

Put the salmon into the pan and turn, coating each side with the seasoned butter mixture. Place salmon, skin side down, in the two pans.

Pour the wine over the salmon and add the chopped scallions and sliced mushrooms.

Cover the pan with baker's paper or aluminum foil and place in the oven for 15 minutes or until fish is opaque and flakes easily with a fork or knife tip, and is pink and still juicy (do not overcook).

To serve, fill a pastry bag with the colcannon and pipe around the edges of 4 dinner plates. Arrange the salmon in the centers of the plates and spoon the pan juices, onions, and mushrooms over the salmon. If desired, decorate the colcannon with sprigs of fresh parsley.

Leeks

The leek is an herb which is a member of the lily family. It has a taste similar to that of an onion, but not as sharp, and is delicious in a variety of dishes, from the above colcannon recipe to soups. However, it is a root plant and gathers a lot of dirt and grit inside the stalk as it grows. The pictures below demonstrate a quick and simple way to clean and chop leeks.

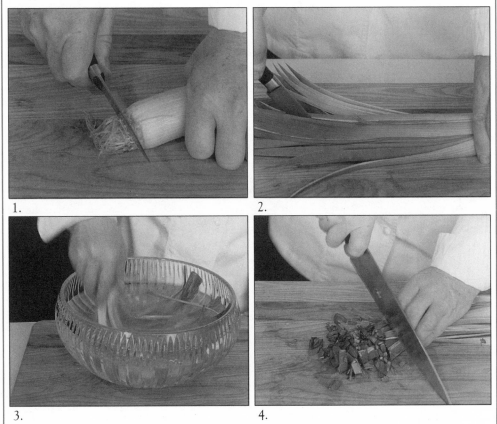

1.) Trim the root from the leek, keeping the end intact. 2.) Slice the leek lengthwise to desired thickness. 3.) Swish the sliced leek in clean water until there is no trace of dirt and grit. 4.) Drain the leek, and chop to desired consistency.

Lamb with Dublin Coddle and Black Currant Sauce

Serves 4

2   whole lamb loins
2   tablespoons vegetable or olive oil
2   teaspoons garlic
2   teaspoons rosemary
2   teaspoons marjoram
    Salt and pepper to taste
2   bunches watercress
    Dublin Coddle (recipe follows)
    Black Currant Sauce (recipe follows)

Preheat oven to 400°.

Rub the lamb loins well with oil, garlic, rosemary, marjoram, salt, and pepper.

Preheat a large, heavy, oven-proof skillet over high heat. Sear the loins on all sides to brown and seal in the juices. Leaving the meat in the skillet, place in oven for 15 minutes (the meat will be medium-rare).

Remove from oven and cut meat into half-inch-thick slices. Fan the lamb slices on dinner plates, along one side of the plate and pour a ribbon of the Black Currant Sauce over the lamb. Spoon the Dublin Coddle onto the opposite side of the plate. Garnish with sprigs of watercress or parsley in the center of the plate between the lamb and the Dublin Coddle.

Dublin Coddle

8   large new potatoes
½   pound sausage (Irish sausage, if available)
½   cup leeks, chopped
2   cups heavy cream
     Salt and pepper
1   scallion, chopped
2   tablespoons prepared horseradish

Scrub potatoes and dice into half-inch cubes, cover with water and bring to boil. Cook until tender and drain.

Slice sausage into half-inch pieces, sauté lightly with the chopped leeks, then add the potatoes.

Add the cream and salt and pepper to taste. Cook until cream reduces in volume and thickens. Stir in the chopped scallion and horseradish and serve.

Black Currant Sauce

¾	cup black currants
½	cup black currant juice
2	tablespoons honey
1	tablespoon Irish whiskey
2	tablespoons crème de cassis liqueur

Warm the black currants, currant juice, and honey over medium heat. Add the whiskey and liqueur. Do not boil.

Spit-Roasted Lemon-Pepper Chicken

Serves 4

1	whole frying chicken, about 3 pounds (preferably free-range)
2	tablespoons olive oil
2	cloves garlic, minced
1 ½	tablespoons Dijon mustard
1	tablespoon lemon pepper
2	teaspoons coarse kosher salt
	Fresh rosemary

Rinse chicken and pat dry. Rub entire surface with oil and crushed garlic. Brush with the Dijon mustard and sprinkle with lemon pepper and salt. Place a few sprigs of rosemary in the cavity of the chicken.

To roast on a spit, cook 40–45 minutes at medium setting, or until done (juices should run clear when the thigh is pierced). Baste occasionally with oil and mustard, and sprinkle with chopped rosemary leaves about 1 minute before removing from the spit.

(For a conventional oven, prepare chicken as above and roast, basting occasionally, at 350° for 40–45 minutes, or until done.)

Filet of Sole Galway Bay

Serves 4

Legendary crooner Bing Crosby familiarized countless Americans with beautiful Galway Bay in Ireland with a song of the same name. This dish was a mainstay at the Hotel Russell where I served as chef's apprentice. I don't know who initiated the recipe, but I assume it was created by the proud and elegant French chef Pierre Roland, who ran the kitchen of the Russell with iron discipline and created an atmosphere where the pursuit of excellence was the norm. (This recipe also works with flounder and orange roughy.)

½   cup plus 5 tablespoons butter or margarine, softened
    Salt and pepper
2   tablespoons lemon juice
1 ½ cups fish stock
8   small filets of sole (about 2 pounds)
4   small shallots, chopped fine
8   fresh mushroom caps, sliced
¾   cup chardonnay
1   cup heavy cream or evaporated skim milk
2   tablespoons grated Gruyère cheese
1   tablespoon chopped fresh parsley
1   tablespoon chopped scallions
8   tablespoons chopped cooked spinach
½   teaspoon nutmeg
¼   teaspoon garlic
3   cups warm mashed potatoes

Coat the bottom of a large baking dish with 4 tablespoons of butter. Sprinkle with salt and pepper to taste and add the lemon juice.

Arrange the fish filets in the dish, turning them to coat with the seasoned butter and lemon juice. Pour the fish stock over the filets and cover with greased baking paper. Bake for 15 minutes at 325°.

While the filets are baking, melt a ½ cup of butter in a saucepan. Add the shallots and cook on high heat for two minutes. Add the mushrooms and continue to cook for another two minutes. Add the chardonnay and continue cooking until liquid is reduced by half.

When fish is done, remove the filets from the oven. Transfer fish to a platter and keep warm. Add the liquid from the baking dish to the butter, mushroom, and wine mixture. Cook over high heat until the contents of the saucepan are reduced by half. Stir in the cream and half the Gruyère cheese and continue cooking for 5 minutes. Remove immediately from the heat and add the parsley and the scallions.

In a small saucepan, melt 1 tablespoon of butter over medium heat. Add the cooked spinach and toss to warm. Add the nutmeg and garlic, and salt and pepper to taste.

With a pastry bag, pipe the warm mashed potatoes around the edges of 4 oven-proof serving plates. Place 2 tablespoons of the spinach in the center of each plate and place the fish on top of the spinach. Spoon the sauce over the fish and sprinkle with Parmesan and the rest of the Gruyère on top. Broil at 500° until cheese turns golden brown.

Note: Fish stock or fish buillon cubes can be purchased in most supermarkets. Be sure to carefully follow package directions if using the buillon cubes. For a fresh alternative, see the glossary for directions for making fish stock.

Irish Whiskey Truffles in Green Peppermint Sauce

Although this is a simple recipe, it needs to be prepared in two steps, the first one about one day in advance. A top-quality chocolate, such as Lindt or Ghirardelli, is necessary for this recipe—chocolate chip morsels will not work, nor will baking chocolate. You also might want to wear plastic food-service gloves for the rolling processes so it is less messy.

Makes 70 truffles

2	cups heavy whipping cream
¼	cup (½ stick) butter
1	pound semisweet chocolate, chopped
1	tablespoon Irish whiskey
2	pounds semisweet chocolate, chopped
	Green Peppermint Sauce (recipe follows)

In a heavy saucepan, heat the cream over medium-high heat just until bubbles appear along the edges (do not boil). Reduce heat to low and stir in the butter and 1 pound of chocolate. Continue stirring, just until chocolate is melted. Add the Irish whiskey and remove from heat. Let cool and cover with plastic wrap. Refrigerate overnight until mixture is dense enough to hold its shape when scooped with a spoon.

Using a spoon or melon scoop, scoop up small amounts of the truffle mixture and roll lightly to make ¾-inch balls. Place truffles on a tray and cover and re-frigerate or freeze for 15 to 20 minutes, until they are very firm.

Place the 2 pounds of chocolate in the top of a double boiler. Place over sim-mering water and warm, stirring constantly, just until the chocolate is about three-fourths melted. (Note: The chocolate should be just warm, not hot. Also, take care that no steam or water gets into the chocolate itself.) Remove choco-late from heat and continue to stir until it is completely melted.

Spread a thin layer of the melted chocolate in the palm of hand (using plas-tic gloves as recommended above). Roll the truffle balls in the melted choco-late, coating just enough to form a thin, light shell. By rolling them between the

Lemon Pepper Shrimp with Herbed Couscous (page 51).

Medallions of Beef with Brandy and Peppercorn Sauce (page 17), accompanied by Potato and Red Pepper Pancakes (page 116).

palms of your hands they will get the wrinkley surface characteristic of the real truffles from which these get their name. (As an alternative, the melted chocolate may be spread on a warm—not hot—plate or pie pan, and roll the truffles lightly. What is important is that they are rolled, not dipped—which would form too thick a coating.) Place truffles on waxed paper-covered tray and chill 30 minutes. If a thicker coating is desired, repeat the coating process, and chill until ready to serve.

Green Peppermint Sauce

1   cup heavy whipping cream
2   tablespoons crème de menthe
    Fresh mint leaves
    Black currants

Whip the cream until soft peaks form, being careful not to overwhip. Add the crème de menthe and fold in carefully.

Spread a pool of the sauce on a dessert plate. Arrange 3 truffles on the sauce and garnish with mint leaves and black currants.

Toasted Pecan Gooseberry Fillo Roll

2 ½   cups chopped pecans

2   cups gooseberries

1 ¼   cups granulated sugar

½   cup water

3   tablespoons maple syrup

¼   cup honey

1   teaspoon cinnamon

¼   cup brown sugar

8   sheets of fillo dough

6   tablespoons (¾ stick) butter, melted

Spread pecans on a baking sheet and toast in a 375° oven for 5 minutes. Set aside.

In a medium saucepan combine the gooseberries, 1 cup of sugar, water, maple syrup, and honey. Cook over medium heat until slightly syrupy. Remove from the heat and stir in the pecans. Set aside to cool.

In a small bowl, mix the remaining ¼ cup of sugar with the cinnamon and brown sugar.

Stack the sheets of fillo and keep covered with a damp towel. Remove one sheet and place it lengthwise on the work surface. Brush the sheet with some melted butter and sprinkle 2 teaspoons of the cinnamon-sugar mixture on top. Place a second sheet of fillo on top of the first. Butter and sugar it. Continue stacking, buttering, and sprinkling until there are four layers of fillo. Repeat the process with the rest of the fillo to make a second stack.

Preheat the oven to 350°.

Spread the gooseberry-pecan mixture in the middle over one of the stacks of fillo. Carefully lift and place the second stack of Fillo on top of the gooseberry-pecan mixture. Starting from one of the short ends, roll the fillo into a cylinder. Tuck the ends of the roll under the bottom. Brush the top with any remaining butter and sprinkle any leftover cinnamon sugar on top. Bake until golden brown, 15 to 20 minutes. Slice and serve warm.

Wasabi and Cheddar Potato Cakes

Wasabi may be found in the Oriental food section of the supermarket.

Serves 5

¼	cup wasabi
	Heavy cream
6	Idaho potatoes, peeled and grated
1	medium onion, diced
3	eggs, beaten
1	teaspoon nutmeg
¼	teaspoon Tabasco sauce
¼	teaspoon each salt and pepper
1 ½	cups flour
½	pound sharp cheddar cheese, grated

Mix the wasabi and just enough cream to give the consistency of creamed horseradish.

Combine the potatoes and onions and place in a large mixing bowl. Add eggs, nutmeg, Tabasco, and salt and pepper. Gradually add flour until thoroughly blended. Add the cheese and wasabi mixture.

Lightly oil a skillet and place over medium-high heat. Drop the potato mixture by quarter-cupfuls into the heated skillet, smoothing slightly with a spoon or spatula to make thin cakes. Sauté to golden brown on each side. Re-oil the skillet as needed.

Stuffed Lobsters Mount Brandan

This dish is named after the highest mountain in Ireland, overlooking the village of Clahan and the beautiful Dingle peninsula of County Kerry. It is a place of long silent summer evenings, winding lanes, deeply peaceful shorelines, and estuaries where swans keep the secrets of a thousand years of myth and legend.

Serves 4

2	whole cooked Maine lobsters
8	ounces crab meat
4	raw clams
4	raw oysters
6	tablespoons (¾ stick) butter or margarine
1	tablespoon lemon juice
2	tablespoons shallots, chopped
1	heaping tablespoon chopped celery
1	cup chardonnay
1	tablespoon each chopped fresh parsley, chopped fresh dill, minced garlic, and chopped fresh basil
¾	cup heavy cream or evaporated skim milk
2	tablespoons grated Parmesan cheese
¾	cup grated mozzarella cheese

Split lobsters from head to tail, and carefully remove the meat and insides, reserving shell halves intact. (With the exception of the tissue around the brain, all of the insides of the lobster are edible and can be saved for use in flavoring sauce or soup.) Crack the claws and remove the meat. Chop the lobster meat into small (quarter-inch) chunks.

Open the clams and oysters and remove the meat from the shells. (If you wish, this may be done by the fish market.)

Preheat a skillet and add the butter or margarine. When it sizzles add the lemon juice. Add the chopped shallots and celery and sauté for two minutes.

Add the mushrooms, garlic, and tomatoes. Cook for two more minutes and add half the wine. Add the oysters, clams, crab meat and lobster. Stir over high heat for 3 minutes, gradually adding the remainer of the wine. Stir in the cream or evaporated milk. Remove from heat and add the fresh herbs.

Preheat broiler to 500°. Stuff the lobster shell halves with the seafood mixture. Sprinkle with mozzarella and Parmesan. Place on a baking sheet and place under broiler just until the cheese turns slightly brown.

Roasted Eggplant and Pepper-Scallion Salad

This is good served warm over fresh spinach greens, or cold over romaine or Bibb lettuce.

Serves 4

2	medium eggplants, peeled and cut in half
1	red pepper
1	yellow pepper
6	plum tomatoes, quartered
¼	olive oil
1	tablespoon coarse kosher salt
1	red onion
1	bunch scallions
½	cup balsamic vinegar
3	tablespoons Dijon mustard
¼	cup crumbled goat cheese

Preheat oven to 475°. Place the eggplant, whole peppers, and tomatoes on a baking sheet. Drizzle all with the olive oil and sprinkle with salt.

Place in oven and roast about 20 minutes or until eggplant is soft and skin on peppers is blackened and soft. Cut the eggplant into cubes. Slip the skin off the peppers, remove the seeds, and chop.

Thinly slice the scallions and red onion, and place in a large bowl. Add the eggplant, peppers, and tomatoes and toss. Combine the mustard and balsamic vinegar and pour over the salad. Sprinkle with goat cheese and serve.

Wild Rice and Turnip Greens Soup

Serves 4

½	cup diced onion
¼	cup chopped celery
1	tablespoon olive oil
2	plum tomatoes, chopped
1	tablespoon sun-dried tomatoes
¼	cup cooked wild rice (see page 88)
1	teaspoon curry powder
1	teaspoon Tabasco sauce
2	cloves garlic, minced
2	teaspoons chopped fresh sage
	Pinch of saffron
	Salt to taste
4	cups hot vegetable broth or water
½	cup chopped turnip greens

Over medium-high heat sauté the onions and celery in the olive oil about 5 minutes, or until the onions are transluscent. Add the chopped plum and dried tomatoes and the cooked wild rice and stir.

Add the curry powder, Tabasco, garlic, sage, saffron, and salt. Stir in the vegetable broth or water; bring just to the boiling point and remove from heat.

Tear the turnip greens into small, bite-sized pieces. Add to the soup and serve immediately.

Spring

April

Farmer Max is the gatekeeper to the green deep summer, showing up every year on a rainy or light spangled April day to inquire about our upcoming produce needs. Today he conjures up a Proustian image of childhood. He reminds me of the picture of a gardener with a barrow full of produce embroidered on a special tablecloth my mother used for afternoon teas in Dublin. Max wears a peaked John Deere cap instead of the straw hat worn by the man on the tablecloth. The wise, relaxed jowls and saucer eyes of an owl recessed in the shade of the cap create a demeanor calmed by a lifetime of early rising.

Max leans on the side of his truck, a stationary lump of Red Man bulging in his right cheek. Arms folded, we squint at each other through the new sun that flutters about us like a drunken butterfly—weak, pale, and deliriously celebrating its own arrival. There are few words and long pauses. We wander in our own thoughts and share in the new light's healing and renewing promise. Max does not so much wear those dark blue dungarees, oversized tee-shirt, and dusty cap, as reside in them like a hobbit in his cavern.

"Do you know what you'll be wantin' this year?" he asks. "I'm puttin' in tamatas, peppers, beans . . ." He stops chewing and scratches his elbow in an exploratory way, as if trying to pin down the location of a few of last year's bug bites.

"How about nasturtiums and baby vegetables?" I respond, just like I do about this time every year.

Sea Bass with Tomato-Kalamata Olive Tapenade

Serves 4

1	cup pitted kalamata olives
¾	cup sun-dried tomatoes
6	anchovy filets
3	tablespoons capers
2	tablespoons chopped fresh basil
3	tablespoons chopped fresh parsley
1	garlic clove, minced
3	tablespoons olive oil
4	8-ounce sea bass filets (1 ½–2 inches thick)
¼	cup olive oil
	Salt and pepper
	Juice of 1 medium lemon
1	cup chardonnay

To make the tapenade, combine the kalamata olives, sun-dried tomatoes, anchovy filets, capers, basil, parsley, and garlic in the bowl of a food processor and process to a smooth paste. Transfer to a mixing bowl and stir in the 3 tablespoons of olive oil.

Preheat oven to 375°. Rub the sea bass with the ¼ cup of olive oil and sprinkle with salt and pepper to taste. Arrange the fish in a baking dish and pour the lemon juice and chardonnay over them. Bake for 15 minutes, or until fish turns opaque and flakes easily.

Arrange the fish on serving plates with a small amount of the tapenade on the side. Pass the rest of the tapenade.

Black Bean Cakes with Marinated Scallions

These are a delicious accompaniment for Spit-Roasted Lemon-Pepper Chicken (page 29).

Serves 4

Marinated scallions

½	cup chopped scallions
¼	cup port wine
1	tablespoon peanut oil
1	tablespoon soy sauce
1	teaspoon minced fresh ginger

Bean Cakes

1	cup dried black beans
4	cups chicken or vegetable broth or water
2	garlic cloves, minced
2	teaspoons Tabasco
1	tablespoon balsamic vinegar
1	tablespoon maple syrup
1	teaspoon nutmeg
1	teaspoon minced fresh ginger
¼	cup shredded jack cheese
¼	cup crumbled goat cheese
	Salt
⅓	cup chopped sun-dried tomatoes

FOR THE MARINATED SCALLIONS: Combine the scallions, port, peanut oil, soy sauce, and ginger. Marinate about 8 hours. (These may be prepared a day ahead.)

FOR THE BEAN CAKES: Rinse the beans and soak in water overnight. Drain the the beans and place in a 4-quart pan. Add the broth or water and bring to a boil. Reduce heat to simmer and cook for about 2 hours, stirring frequently, until beans are done. (The beans will burst and have a tender, pasty consistency when done. Add more liquid as needed while cooking to prevent beans from scorching or sticking.)

Add the balsamic vinegar, maple syrup, garlic, nutmeg, ginger, Tabasco, and salt to taste. Simmer and stir for 5 minutes. Add the cheeses, dried tomatoes, and marinated scallions. Let the mixture cool. (It should be thick and pasty.)

Shape the mixture into small patties or cakes and sauté in a lightly oiled skillet, about 5 minutes on each side.

Walden Inn Power Salad

Serves 4

Salad

6	new red potatoes
1/3	cup artichokes hearts
2	fresh tomatoes, chopped
1	cup asparagus tips
1	cup fresh torn spinach
1	tablespoon dried tomatoes
8	anchovy filets (optional)
1	tablespoon chopped fresh chives
3	tablespoons chopped kalamata olives
2	teaspoons minced garlic
1/2	cup crumbled goat cheese

Vinaigrette

3/4	cup balsamic vinegar
1/4	cup olive oil
	Salt and pepper to taste

Steam or boil the potatoes until tender. Let cool and cut into ½-inch slices. Steam or boil the asparagus tips just until tender. Combine the potatoes and asparagus tips with the rest of the salad ingredients. Whisk together the vinaigrette ingredients and toss with the salad.

Crab and Oyster Pasta Salad

Serves 4

2   cups penne pasta
½   cup olive oil
1   teaspoon minced garlic
2   tablespoons chopped fresh cilantro
2   tablespoons chopped sun-dried tomatoes
½   cup chardonnay
12   oysters, shucked
8   ounces crab meat
2   tablespoons Parmesan
1   tablespoon chopped fresh parsley

Cook the penne pasta in 1 quart boiling water just until it is *al dente*. Drain and set aside.

In a bowl, combine the olive oil, garlic, cilantro, and tomatoes.

In a saucepan, bring the oysters and chardonnay to a simmer and cook for 5 minutes.

Combine crabmeat, oysters, and dressing, and toss with the pasta. Sprinkle with Parmesan and chopped parsley and serve.

Black Bean, Tomato, and Mushroom Timbales

More than a garnish, but not quite a side dish, these wonderful "accompaniments" are excellent served with grilled chicken or fish.

Serves 4

1   cup cooked black beans
⅓   cup diced fresh tomatoes
½   tablespoon chopped sun-dried tomatoes
¼   cup chopped scallions
¼   cup mushroom caps, chopped
2   egg whites
     Salt and pepper

Grease the insides of four 2-ounce timbale molds (or any type of two- or three-ounce oven-proof baking molds or dishes).

In a large bowl, mix all ingredients. Season with salt and pepper to taste.

Fill the molds with the mixture and arrange in a shallow baking pan. Add enough boiling water to come one-third up the sides of the timbales. Bake at 375° for 15 minutes. Remove molds from the water bath and allow to dry briefly on a towel. Gently loosen sides of the timbales with a knife and turn upside down on plates.

Linguine with Spinach and Toasted Walnuts

Serves 4

¼   cup walnut halves
4   tablespoons olive oil
2   cups fresh torn spinach (not packed)
¼   pound pancetta, diced in ¼-inch pieces
3   garlic cloves, minced
2   cups chicken broth
½   teaspoon coarse kosher salt
1   teaspoon crushed red pepper
½   cup asiago cheese, grated
   Linguine (for 4 servings)

Spread the walnuts on a baking sheet and toast in a 375° oven for 5 minutes. Set aside.

Heat the olive oil and sauté spinach, garlic, and pancetta over medium heat for 8–10 minutes. Increase heat to high and add the chicken broth. Cook until liquid is reduced by half, and add salt and crushed red pepper.

Cook linguine according to package directions, until *al dente*. Drain and toss with a little olive oil.

Toss the cooked linguine with the sauce. Add the asiago cheese and toasted walnuts and serve.

Artichoke and Mixed Green Salad

Serves 6

1	bunch romaine lettuce, washed and torn in bite-sized pieces
1	head Boston or Bibb lettuce, washed
½	cup drained artichoke hearts
1	yellow tomato, sliced
1	red tomato, sliced
½	cup crumbled goat cheese
2	tablespoons Dijon mustard
1	teaspoon cider vinegar
1	tablespoon chardonnay
1	cup walnut oil
1	clove garlic, minced
3	teaspoons chopped fresh basil
1	tablespoon chopped fresh thyme
1	teaspoon salt
1	teaspoon pepper
2	cups balsamic vinegar
½	cup grated asiago cheese

Toss the romaine lettuce with the artichoke hearts, tomatoes, and goat cheese.

Combine the next ten ingredients and blend well.

Arrange leaves of Boston or Bibb lettuce in salad bowls and place the salad on top. Drizzle with the dressing, sprinkle with the asiago cheese, and serve.

Cherry Walnut Tart

Makes a 9-inch tart

1   cup walnut pieces
¼   cup melted butter
2   cups crushed graham cracker crumbs
⅓   cup sugar
¼   cup cornstarch
4   cups pitted sweet cherries
¼   teaspoon salt
3   tablespoons butter or margarine, melted

Spread the walnuts on a baking sheet and toast in a 375° oven for 5 minutes. Finely chop the walnuts.

Combine ½ cup of the walnuts and the graham cracker crumbs. Add the melted butter and press the mixture into a 9-inch tart pan.

Combine the remaining walnuts, sugar, and cornstarch in the bowl of a food processor and blend until the nuts are pulverized.

In a large bowl combine the cherries with the sugar-nut mixture and salt. Mix well. Pile the cherry mixture into the crust and dot with the 3 tablespoons of butter.

Bake at 375° for 25 minutes, then reduce the heat to 350° and bake about 35 minutes longer, until the juices are bubbling.

Pan-fried Trout with Papaya-Avocado Salsa

Serves 4

⅓   cup olive oil
¼   cup chardonnay
2   teaspoons cayenne
1   teaspoon cracked black pepper
4   boneless trout filets
1   cup diced papaya
¼   cup lime juice
1   small red onion, peeled and sliced
1   red pepper, seeded and diced
2   cloves garlic, minced
1   medium avocado
1   cup flour
2   teaspoons salt
2   tablespoons olive oil

Mix the ⅓ cup of olive oil with the chardonnay, cayenne, and black pepper in a shallow pan. Marinate the trout in the mixture in the refrigerator for 1 hour.

To make the salsa, combine the papaya, lime juice, onion, red pepper, and garlic. Refrigerate for 1 hour. Just before serving, peel, seed, and chop the avocado and add to the salsa. (Avocado discolors and darkens when exposed to the air for too long.)

Combine the flour and salt. Remove the trout from the marinade and dredge with the flour. Heat the 2 tablespoons of olive oil in a skillet over medium-high heat and sauté the trout, about 6 minutes. Turn and sauté for another 6 minutes, or until fish turns opaque.

While the trout cooks, peel and chop the avocado and add to the salsa. Serve the fish with the salsa on the side.

May,

bursting with the resurrected glory of warmer weather, brings a full menu of events rich in ritual and celebration to our college campus location. The Inn has absorbed these memories over the years like a faithful old family box camera, stacking the snapshots in the shoe box of its spirit: Mother's day and graduation receptions, wine tastings on the porches and in tents on the lawn, catered champagne suppers under the covered bridge by Cataract Falls, garnishing classes under the gingko tree in the university quadrangle, poetry readings in the James Whitcomb Riley Library, and recitals in Thompson Hall, the college's performing arts center.

Food undergoes a final transition in lightness that began at the end of March. Indulgence in calories gives way to indulgence in clothes before June arrives to make a rumpled mockery of the most delicate outfits, prompting delicacies like poached salmon of pastel pink. A ribbon of lemon-yellow chardonnay, caper, and chive sauce, and translucent little new potatoes carved in the shape of plover's eggs with asparagus in red pepper rings complement this dish.

May is a rush to plant a hundred flower boxes with pansies, petunias, impatiens, and vining vinca and to mulch the hill of colorful perennials in the back of the Inn. These are our efforts to provide a suitable backdrop to the parade of caps and gowns that bustle with such excitement, such elegance, such promise, and such hope on their way to life's fulfillment.

Gratin of Seafood Mediterranean

Serves 4

4   shallots, minced

3   fresh plum tomatoes, chopped

2   tablespoons chopped sun-dried tomatoes

6   pitted kalamata olives, cut in quarters

¼   cup olive oil

8   ounces crab meat

8   medium shrimp, peeled and deveined

8   clams, shelled

1   large red pepper, roasted, peeled, seeded, and sliced (page 52)

½   cup quartered artichoke bottoms

⅓   cup balsamic vinegar

2   teaspoons minced garlic

1   tablespoon Dijon mustard

½   teaspoon pepper

2   tablespoons crumbled goat cheese

1   tablespoon grated Parmesan

Sauté the shallots over medium heat in 1 teaspoon of the olive oil for 3 minutes. Add the fresh and dried tomatoes, olives, and seafood and continue to sauté for another 5 minutes. Add the red pepper.

Add all remaining ingredients except the cheese, and continue cooking for 5 minutes, stirring occasionally.

Spoon into a casserole dish or four individual ramekins and sprinkle with crumbled goat cheese and Parmesan and bake at 350° for 10 minutes or until cheese is slightly crusted.

Lemon Pepper Shrimp on Herbed Couscous

Serves 4

3 ¼ cups water or broth

½ teaspoon salt

2 cups couscous

2 tablespoons fresh chopped basil

½ teaspoon chopped fresh sage

½ teaspoon chopped fresh rosemary

½ teaspoon anise

24 medium fresh shrimp, peeled and deveined

3 ½ tablespoons olive oil

1 teaspoon minced garlic

1 ½ teaspoons lemon pepper

1 teaspoon coriander

1 teaspoon paprika

Heat the water or broth and salt to boiling. Stir in the couscous; cover and remove from the heat and let stand for 6 minutes. Add the basil, sage, rosemary, and anise and fluff with a fork.

Pack the couscous into 4 small oiled ramekin or soufflé cups. Unmold the couscous onto the centers of serving plates.

Toss the shrimp with the next 5 ingredients. Sauté the coated shrimp over medium-high heat until they turn opaque in color (about 10 minutes). Arrange around the couscous timbales and serve.

New Potato and Artichoke Salad

Serves 4

8	large new potatoes, steamed or boiled
1 ½	cups artichoke hearts, coarsely chopped
1	cup balsamic vinegar
½	cup olive oil
1	tablespoon paprika
1	tablespoon chopped fresh marjoram
1	scant tablespoon minced garlic
2	tablespoons Dijon mustard
2	tablespoons Worcestershire sauce
	Salt and pepper to taste

Quarter the potatoes and add the artichokes. Combine the rest of the ingredients and mix with the potatoes and artichokes.

Roasted Peppers

Several recipes in this book, such as the following one for Pecan-Encrusted Amberjack, call for roasted red and/or yellow bell peppers. Although roasted peppers can be found in supermarkets (in the section with the pickles), the technique for roasting them yourself is fairly simple.

Hold the pepper over an open flame (such as on a gas stove or barbecue grill), or broil just until the skin turns black. Wrap the pepper in plastic wrap for 5 minutes. The skin will then slip right off, and the pepper can be seeded and sliced or diced, as desired.

Pecan Encrusted Amberjack with Mango, Pepper, and Black Bean Salsa

Serves 6

2	large red peppers, roasted, peeled, and seeded (see page 52)
1	mango, peeled and pitted
½	cup cooked black beans
1	cup chopped fresh cilantro
½	cup chopped red onion
2	tablespoons fresh lime juice
1	tablespoon olive oil
1	tablespoon balsamic vinegar
1	teaspoon minced garlic
¼	teaspoon cayenne pepper
½	teaspoon salt
3	cups pecans
6	amberjack filets (about 6 ounces each)
½	cup all-purpose flour
2	large eggs, beaten
4	tablespoons vegetable oil

For the salsa, dice the pepper and mango into quarter-inch pieces. Combine the pepper and mango with the next 9 ingredients in a saucepan and warm over medium heat.

Place the pecans in the bowl of a food processor and process just until they resemble a coarse meal. (Be careful not to overprocess or they will become pasty.)

Lightly dust the amberjack filets with flour. Dip the fish into the beaten eggs and then lightly coat with the ground pecans.

Heat the vegetable oil in a skillet over high heat. Add the coated amberjack and sauté 2 minutes per side, until brown. Transfer the fish to a baking sheet and place in a preheated 350° oven for 8 minutes, or until fish is opaque and flakes easily.

Serve either on a bed of the warm salsa or with the salsa on the side.

Eggplant and Cheese Torte with Tomato-Basil Salsa

Serves 4

1	cup chopped fresh peeled and seeded tomatoes
¼	cup chopped fresh basil
2	teaspoons minced garlic
¼	cup balsamic vinegar
2	teaspoons salt
1 ½	teaspoons pepper
2	medium eggplants
½	cup balsamic vinegar
1	cup grated mozzarella cheese
½	cup Gruyère cheese
2	tablespoons grated Parmesan cheese

To make the salsa, combine the first 6 ingredients. Set aside.

Thinly slice the eggplant lengthwise (about ⅛ inch thick) and grill the slices.

Lightly grease a 9-inch springform pan. Cover the bottom of the pan with a layer of overlapping slices of the grilled eggplant. Brush or sprinkle the balsamic vinegar on the eggplant slices and top with a little of the salsa. Combine all 3 cheeses and evenly sprinkle a layer of the mix over the salsa.

Continue the layering process until you have several layers and all the ingredients are used. Preheat oven to 375° and bake the torte for 10 minutes or until the cheese melts.

Remove the sides of the pan, cut the torte in wedges and serve.

Lemon Poppy Seed Bread

Makes 3 loaves

4 ¼   cups all-purpose flour
¼   teaspoons salt
1   tablespoon baking powder
½   cup instant lemon pudding mix
1   cup (2 sticks) butter, softened
3   cups sugar
6   eggs
1 ½   cups milk
       Juice of 3 lemons
2   teaspoons lemon extract
¾   cup poppyseeds

Grease and flour three 8 x 4-inch loaf pan. Preheat oven to 350°.

Sift together the flour, salt, baking powder, and pudding mix in a large mixing bowl.

In a large bowl cream the butter and the sugar, beating until light and fluffy.

In another bowl beat together the eggs, milk, lemon juice, and extract.

Alternately add the dry ingredients and the egg and milk mixture to the creamed butter and sugar, stirring just enough to blend the ingredients. Do not overmix. Fold in the poppy seeds.

Scoop the batter into the prepared loaf pans and bake 40–45 minutes or until done. Place on a wire rack and allow to cool in pans for 15 minutes. Remove from pans and finish cooling on a wire rack.

Purée of Scallop and Red Pepper Bisque

Designed for the more experienced—or adventurous—cook, this recipe involves incorporating the puréed scallops with the liquid without having the scallops congeal. It's tricky, but it can be mastered with some practice.

Serves 6

¾ cup bay scallops, uncooked and well chilled
4 red peppers, roasted, peeled, and seeded (page 52)
3 ½ cups cold vegetable broth, fish stock, or water
6 shallots, chopped
1 tablespoon olive oil
2 cloves garlic, minced
¼ cup chardonnay
½ teaspoon nutmeg
1 teaspoon Tabasco
½ teaspoon coriander
¼ teaspoon saffron
Tomato, Eggplant, and Caper Salsa (recipe follows)

In a food processor, purée the scallops and the peppers together. Add the cold broth, stock, or water a little at a time.

In a large saucepan, sauté the shallots in the olive oil for 5 minutes. Add the garlic, chardonnay, nutmeg, Tabasco, and coriander. Cook until liquid is reduced by half. Remove from heat and cool to lukewarm.

Add the scallop mixture to the pan with the shallots and spices. Heat over low heat just to the boiling point, whisking constantly to prevent the the mixture from congealing. Add the saffron and whisk until well blended. Serve in wide soup bowls with a dollop of the salsa.

Tomato, Eggplant, and Caper Salsa

4 plum tomatoes, chopped
1 small eggplant, peeled and diced
2 cloves garlic, whole and unpeeled
½ teaspoon anise
1 ½ teaspoons olive oil

1 ½ teaspoons honey
¼   cup balsamic vinegar
8   leaves fresh basil, chopped
1   tablespoon capers

Combine tomatoes, eggplant, garlic, anise, and olive oil in a shallow baking dish and bake at 275° for 30 minutes. Combine the honey and vinegar and add to the mixture. Bake another 5 minutes.

Remove the garlic cloves. Peel and crush them and return the garlic to the mixture. Add the basil and capers. (This can be made one day ahead.)

Shrimp and Scallops in a Leek Broth

Serves 6

1   small onion, diced
2   garlic cloves, minced
1   tablespoon olive oil
½   cup chardonnay
1   leek, white part only, thinly sliced
½   cup fish stock
1   cup clam juice
6   medium raw shrimp, peeled, deveined, and sliced in half
1   cup bay scallops
1   cup heavy cream or evaporated skim milk
1   teaspoon Tabasco sauce
1   teaspoon salt

In a large pan, sauté onion and garlic in the olive oil over medium-high heat until onion is transluscent. Add the chardonnay and leek and cook until the liquid is reduced to one-third.

Add the fish stock and clam juice and bring just to boiling (a one-bubble boil). Reduce heat to low and add the scallops and shrimp. Simmer just until seafood turns opaque, about 6 minutes. Do not overcook. Add the cream, Tabasco, and salt. Serve immediately.

Sesame Soba Noodle Salad with Shrimp

Serves 4

1	medium-sized carrot, julienne-sliced
½	pound snow peas
2	tablespoons peanut oil
16	medium raw shrimp, peeled and deveined
3	tablespoons fresh minced ginger
1	7 ½-ounce package sesame soba noodles*
¼	cup sesame oil
½	cup soy sauce
3	tablespoons sesame seeds
1	tablespoon brown sugar
2	teaspoons Tabasco

Bring 2 cups of water to a boil in a medium-sized saucepan. Add the julienned carrots and partially cook, about 3 minutes. Remove carrots with slotted spoon and drain on paper toweling. Place the snow peas in the boiling water and cook for 1 ½ minutes. Remove peas and drain.

Heat the peanut oil in a skillet over medium heat. Add shrimp and sauté for 5 minutes. Add the ginger and continue to sauté another 5 minutes, or until shrimp are opaque.

Cook noodles according to package instructions. Drain well and place in bowl. Toss with the sesame oil, soy sauce, sesame seeds, brown sugar, and Tabasco. Add the shrimp mixture and serve.

* Available in the Oriental foods sections of most grocery stores.

June

and the Midwest are hooped in a halo of blue again.

With May's hectic schedule behind us and the DePauw students departed, Summer settles down with a comfortable yawn over Walden Inn of Greencastle. There will be plenty of coach tours, weddings, and reunions to keep the Inn busy, but there will also be enough wiggle room to allow the staff to begin taking vacations or undertake creative projects.

Eldon, one of our maintenance men and a master carpenter, might use the extra time to put together a length of picket fence. If I ask him nicely, he might even work on another piece of furniture for the lobby. I like to watch his hands as he works with wood. They are concrete, square and open. Oak boards slip into those hands with the ease of a simple truth.

A good chef's work will linger like a fine wine on the memory of the taste buds, but Eldon's work will elicit a quiet nod of respect and admiration when we are no longer here, from people who have not yet visited.

Blueberry Lemon Bread

Makes 3 loaves

4 ½   cups all-purpose flour
1   tablespoon baking powder
1   cup instant lemon pudding mix
¾   teaspoon salt
1   cup (2 sticks) butter, softened
3   cups sugar
6   large eggs
2   tablespoons grated lemon peel
2   cups milk
1 ½   cups blueberries

Grease and flour three 8 x 4-inch loaf pan. Preheat oven to 350°.

Sift together the flour, baking powder, and salt in a bowl.

In a large bowl cream the butter and sugar, beating until light and fluffy. Add eggs one at a time, beating well after each addition. Add lemon peel.

Alternately add the dry ingredients and the milk to the creamed butter and egg mixture, stirring just enough to blend the ingredients. Do not overmix. Fold in the blueberries.

Scoop the batter into the prepared loaf pans and bake for 45–50 minutes or until done. Place on a wire rack and allow to cool in the pans on a wire rack for 15 minutes. Remove the loaves from the pans and finish cooling on the wire rack.

Ebb Tide Harvest

This name was inspired by the shores of western Ireland.

Serves 4

½ cup (1 stick) butter or margarine
    Juice of 1 lemon
12   medium-sized fresh shrimp, peeled and deveined
8   ounces crab meat
8   shucked oysters (optional)
12   medium mushroom caps, sliced
2   fresh tomatoes, chopped
2   teaspoons chopped sun-dried tomatoes
2   teaspoons chopped fresh cilantro
24   leaves fresh spinach, washed and torn
1   cup chardonnay
1   cup cream or evaporated skim milk
4   tablespoons sour cream
4   thin slices Swiss or mozzarella cheese
2   cups cooked rice
2   tablespoons grated Parmesan cheese

Preheat a saucepan or skillet. Add the butter and when it sizzles add the lemon juice. Add the shrimp, crabmeat, and oysters, and cook for one minute.

Add the mushrooms, the fresh and dried tomatoes, and cilantro and cook for one more minute. Add the spinach leaves and chardonnay and cook for one more minute. Add the cream and cook one minute more.

Preheat oven to 350°. Divide the rice among four individual-sized casserole dishes or ramekins. Spoon the seafood mixture over the rice and top each with 1 tablespoon of the sour cream and a slice of cheese. Sprinkle with the Parmesan cheese and bake for 10 minutes or until cheese is brown and bubbly on top.

Mushroom Caps Stuffed with Hummus

If time is a constraint you can find prepared hummus at many delicatessans and supermarkets.

Serves 4–6

1	15-ounce can of chickpeas
½	cup tahini*
2	garlic cloves, minced
¼	cup lemon juice
	Salt and pepper
24	large fresh mushrooms
½	cup chardonnay
¼	cup dry vermouth
	Juice from ½ a lemon
1	tablespoon peanut oil
½	each red and yellow bell peppers, finely diced

To make the hummus, drain the chickpeas, reserving the liquid. In the bowl of a food processor, combine the chickpeas, tahini, garlic, and lemon juice. Purée until smooth.

Season with salt and pepper to taste to taste and thin as needed with the drained chickpea liquid (the mixture should be easily spreadable, but not runny).

Rinse and clean the mushrooms under running water. Remove the stems and reserve for another use, if desired.

Heat the chardonnay, vermouth, lemon juice, and peanut oil in a skillet. Add the mushrooms to the heated liquid and cook until the mushrooms lose their firmness and take on a malleable texture, about 10 minutes. Remove from heat and allow the mushroom caps to cool in the liquid.

Using a large-tipped pastry bag, fill the mushroom caps with hummus.

Sprinkle the diced peppers confetti-style on the stuffed mushrooms and serve.

* Tahini can be found in Middle Eastern food shops or in the ethnic section of the supermarket.

Citrus-Scented Gravlax

Serves 10–12

1   3- to 5-pound salmon filet

1   cup coarse kosher salt

1   pound brown sugar

1   tablespoon white pepper

2   tablespoons brandy

     Juice and zest of one orange

     Juice and zest of one lime

3   tablespoons olive oil

1   cup chopped fresh dill

Combine the salt, sugar and pepper. Set aside.

Place the salmon filet skin-side down on a double layer of cheesecloth. Combine brandy, juices, and olive oil and pour over the salmon, coating the fish well. Sprinkle the orange and lime zests over the fish, and then cover with the dill.

Pack the salt mixture over the salmon, being sure to completely cover the fish. Wrap the cheesecloth tightly around the fish, and then wrap securely with plastic wrap. Perforate the plastic with a fork so that excess juices can escape.

Place the wrapped fish skin-side down on the drip rack of a broiler pan, with the pan underneath. Place weights on the fish to press the juices out. (Bricks or canned goods will work; placing the weights on a sturdy plate or tray helps distribute the weight evenly.) Refrigerate 2 to 3 days.

Unwrap filet and completely rinse away the cure. Using a very sharp knife, slice very thinly on the bias and serve with Irish Brown Soad Bread (page 25), bagels, or toast, accompanied with cream cheese, tomatoes, and onions or scallions.

Grilled Salmon Salad with Black Currant Vinaigrette

Serves 4

1   pound fresh salmon filet, cut in 4 pieces
⅓   cup black currant vinegar (balsamic vinegar may be substituted)
1   tablespoon honey
2   tablespoons cassis liqueur
1   tablespoon Dijon mustard
⅓   cup olive oil
½   cup black currants
4   cups loosely packed torn romaine lettuce
1   cup loosely packed torn fresh spinach

Coat the salmon with a little olive oil. Season with salt and pepper to taste. Grill skin-side down for 10–12 minutes.

Meanwhile, combine the vinegar, honey, liqueur, and Dijon mustard. Add the olive oil and whisk gently just until blended (do not whisk too much or the mixture will become cloudy). Add the black currants.

Toss the lettuce and spinach with just enough dressing to dampen. Divide the salad among 4 individual salad bowls or plates. Place the salmon on top drizzle with some of the remaining dressing.

Sautéed Stuffed Artichoke Hearts

Serves 4

8   artichoke hearts
½   cup mascarpone cheese
½   cup gorgonzola cheese
½   cup chopped sun-dried tomatoes
1   tablespoon lemon juice
½   cup flour
2   eggs, beaten
½   cup cornmeal

Combine the mascarpone, gorgonzola, and lemon juice in a blender and blend until smooth. Transfer cheese mixture to a bowl and add tomatoes.

Gently open the tops of the artichoke hearts, and using a teaspoon, gently press the mixture into the artichoke hearts.

Dust the artichokes with flour, dip in the beaten egg, and dredge in cornmeal. Sauté in a lightly oiled skillet over medium heat and serve.

Spinach, Tomato, and Basil Bruschetta

Serves 4

3   cups washed and torn fresh spinach (not pressed or packed)
2   large or 3 small plum tomatoes
⅓   cup chopped dried tomatoes
1   teaspoon minced garlic
½   teaspoon nutmeg
⅓   cup chopped fresh basil
½   cup chardonnay
⅓   cup plus 1 tablespoon olive oil
¾   cup gorgonzola cheese
8   bias-sliced pieces of french bread, ½ inch thick

Chop the plum tomatoes into quarter-inch pieces.

Sauté the spinach in 1 tablespoon of olive oil over medium heat until it becomes wilted. Add the dried and plum tomatoes, garlic, nutmeg, and basil to the spinach and continue cooking for 3 minutes. Combine the chardonnay and ⅓ cup of olive oil and pour over the spinach mixture. Cook until liquid is evaporated. The mixture should still be very moist.

With tongs, distribute the mixture evenly over the toasted french bread slices and crumble the gorgonzola over the top. Place under a broiler until the cheese is slightly melted, about 2 minutes.

Pesto, Goat Cheese, and Tomato Croutons

Croutons can be more than toasted bread cubes. These are excellent with salads and soups.

Serves 4

4   tablespoons crumbled goat cheese
2   level tablespoons chopped sundried tomatoes
2   level tablespoons chopped scallions
2   English muffins, split
4   teaspoons pesto

Mix the cheese, tomatoes, and scallions. Toast muffin halves and spread with pesto. Top with the cheese-tomato-scallion mixture and bake at 350° for 5 minutes.

Cut each muffin half into 4 pie-shaped wedges and serve.

Little Miss Muffet Cake

Serves 8 to 10

5   egg yolks
3   large eggs
2 ¾   cups granulated sugar
¼   cup brown sugar
½   cup plus 3 tablespoons of freshly squeezed lemon juice
2   teaspoons lemon extract
2   cups sifted cake flour
2   teaspoons finely grated lemon peel
½   teaspoon salt
1   tablespoon baking powder
½   cup unsalted butter, softened
      Whites of 6 large eggs

2   tablespoons confectioners sugar

1   tablespoon cinnamon

In a medium mixing bowl, whisk together the egg yolks, eggs, and ½ cup of the granulated sugar. Stir in ½ cup of the lemon juice.

Put the egg mixture in the top of a double boiler and heat over simmering water. Whisking constantly, cook the mixture until thick, about 10 minutes. Remove from the heat and strain the mixture (called a curd) through a sieve to remove any lumps. (Be sure the outside of the pan is dry so that no water from condensation gets into the curd.) Place a piece of plastic wrap directly on the surface of the mixture to prevent a skin from forming. Let cool and refrigerate until cold.

Sift together the cake flour, ¾ cup of sugar, the salt, baking powder, and brown sugar. Set aside.

In a large mixing bowl, combine the lemon curd, butter, lemon zest, and lemon extract, mixing well. Stir in the dry ingredients until well blended and smooth.

Preheat the oven to 325°. Grease and flour a 9-inch cake pan.

With an electric mixer, whip the egg whites on medium speed until frothy. Increase speed to high and gradually add the remaining 1 ½ cups of granulated sugar. Whip until soft peaks form.

Fold the egg whites into the cake batter. Spread the cake batter in the cake pan.

Bake about 50–55 minutes until top springs back when lightly touched, or tester comes out clean. Cool about 30 minutes and remove the cake from the pan. Cool thoroughly on a wire rack. (The cake can be made a day in advance. Cover with plastic wrap and store at room temperature.)

Combine the confectioners sugar and cinnamon. Sprinkle over the cake and serve.

Summer

July

in Putnam county is an acquired taste. It has certain elements in common with the swims I used to take in the Irish Sea as a boy, done not so much for the teeth-chattering experience itself, but for the subsequent feeling of well-being that came from being fully clothed and warm afterwards.

It is the same kind of impulse that inspires a jog down the country roads about the Inn in the broiling sun in order to experience the sensation of sweet, fresh water from a fountain dousing a head and neck already drunk on the wine of its endorphins.

July also inspires a menu that is liquid, light, and healthful. I think we must have tried every fruit and herb soup combination possible along with a myriad of crunchy salads with citrusy dressings. Experiments in new juice combinations take place with reckless abandon in the kitchen: plums, celery, carrots, jicama, oranges, lemons, limes, kiwis, peaches, grapes, apples, strawberries, raspberries, and blackberries with yogurt and ice cream, are tossed in the juicer in a multiplicity of combinations in an attempt to quench the thirst, energize the metabolism, and rouse a drowsy appetite.

Zucchini, Dried Tomato, Spinach, and Gorgonzola Pie

A robust cabernet or merlot enhances the Mediterranean flavor of this dish.

Serves 4 (or 8, if used as an appetizer)

1 ¼ cups all-purpose flour
½ cup (1 stick) butter or margarine, chilled and cut in small pieces
2 tablespoons cold water
¾ cup thinly sliced zucchini
1 tablespoon olive oil
1 cup loosely packed torn fresh spinach
½ cup crumbled gorgonzola cheese
⅓ cup chopped sun-dried tomatoes
1 small garlic clove, minced
¼ teaspoon nutmeg
Salt and pepper

With a pastry blender or your fingers, work the butter or margarine gently into the flour. Add cold water a bit at a time, just until dough forms a ball. Cover the dough and refrigerate it for 45 minutes.

On a lightly floured surface, roll the dough into a 10-inch round. Gently ease the dough into a lightly oiled 9-inch spring-form pan, forming a half-inch rim.

Preheat oven to 375°. Line the dough with foil and place pie weights on the foil. Bake for 15 minutes or until golden. Carefully remove the foil and weights.

Grill the zucchini slices for 5 minutes on each side. Heat the olive oil in a skillet over medium-high heat. Add the spinach, garlic, and nutmeg and sauté for 5 minutes. Add salt and pepper to taste.

Spread the spinach on the bottom of the baked pastry shell. Sprinkle the dried tomatoes and half the gorgonzola cheese over the spinach. Layer on the zucchini slices pinwheel-fashion and lightly brush with olive oil. Sprinkle the remaining gorgonzola over the zucchini and bake at 350° for 5 minutes. Slice and serve.

Putnam County Fair Queen Pie

Start this dessert the night before because the filling, called a ganache, needs at least 8 hours in the refrigerator in order to thicken properly.

Serves 8 to 10

1	10-inch baked pie shell
1	tablespoon finely diced dried apricots
¼	cup Grand Marnier
14	ounces semisweet chocolate, chopped
2	cups heavy cream
1	tablespoon strawberry preserves
½	tablespoon flaked coconut
1	tablespoon sugar

Soak the dried apricots in the Grand Marnier while preparing the filling.

Place the chocolate in the top of a double boiler and heat over simmering water just until the chocolate melts.

Heat 1 cup of the cream just to the point of boiling. Remove immediately from heat and blend with the melted chocolate. Drain the apricots and add the Grand Marnier to the chocolate and cream mixture and blend well.

Spread the preserves on the insides of the pie shell, and arrange the soaked apricots and coconut flakes over the preserves. Pour the warm ganache over the apricots and coconut, and refrigerate. (The ganache will thicken as it cools.)

Add the sugar to the remaining cream and whip it lightly. Using a pastry bag, pipe the whipped cream over the ganache, or simply dollop it on.

Grilled Bluegills with Chili Tartar Sauce

Bluegills are a small fish found in every lake and pond in Indiana, and hardly a Hoosier has grown up without catching at least a few. This recipe is best when cooked on an outdoor grill.

Serves 4

8	whole bluegills, cleaned and dressed
2	tablespoons corn oil
	Juice of 1 ½ lemons
4	cloves garlic, minced
	Salt and pepper
1	cup mayonnaise
8	teaspoons chili powder
2	teaspoons Tabasco sauce
4	teaspoons Dijon mustard
3	teaspoons Worcestershire sauce
3	tablespoons pickle relish or capers

Cut one or two diagonal slashes across the fish and with oil, lemon juice, and garlic, and sprinkle with salt and pepper to taste.

Place the fish on an oiled rack on a hot preheated grill. Cook about 3 minutes per side, turning once (do not overcook). Flesh should be opaque and flake easily when a knife is inserted.

Combine the remaining 6 ingredients to make the Chili Tartar Sauce, and serve with the grilled fish.

Fresh Fruit with Champagne Sabayon

Serves 4

	Fresh strawberries, raspberries, blueberries, and blackberries (or any seasonal fruit)
3	egg yolks
	Juice of a medium lemon
1	tablespoon sugar

1   tablespoon champagne (sherry may be substituted)

½   cup (1 stick) butter, melted

In a stainless steel mixing bowl, whisk together the egg yolks, lemon juice, sugar, and champagne (a balloon whisk works best).

Set the bowl in a large pan of hot water over low heat. Whisk briskly until the mixture is fluffy, about 5–10 minutes.

Remove from the heat and, whisking constantly, slowly pour the melted butter into the mixture.

Spoon into individual serving dishes and top with the fresh fruit.

Buttermilk Pike Potato Salad

Serves 4

8   small red potatoes

1   cup balsamic vinegar

⅓   cup olive oil

⅓   cup chopped scallions

⅓   cup chopped mushroom caps

⅓   cup bacon bits

2   fresh tomatoes, peeled and chopped

1   teaspoon minced garlic

½   teaspoon nutmeg

½   teaspoon minced fresh ginger

⅓   cup fresh parsley, chopped

1   heaping teaspoon paprika

    Salt and pepper to taste

Steam or boil the potatoes until they are soft all the way through.

Drain the liquid from the potatoes and allow them to dry in their own heat (do not cool with cold water). Dice the potatoes into ½-inch cubes.

Place the rest of the ingredients in a large bowl. Add the potatoes and stir gently until they are thoroughly coated in all of the ingredients.

Orange Ginger Chicken

Serves 6

4	5-ounce boneless, skinless chicken breasts
3	cups orange juice
1	cup chicken broth or water
3	cinnamon sticks
1	tablespoon star anise
1	2-inch piece fresh ginger, peeled and minced
¼	cup mushroom soy sauce
¼	cup Shao-Hsing wine or dry sherry
1	teaspoon arrowroot
1	tablespoon water

In a large saucepan, combine the orange juice, broth or water, cinnamon sticks, star anise, and ginger. Bring just to a boil over high heat. Add the mushroom soy sauce and return to a boil. Reduce heat to low and simmer for 20 minutes.

Add the wine and bring to a boil again. Add the chicken breasts and return to a boil. Reduce heat to low, cover and simmer for 15 minutes. Remove from heat and let the chicken stand in the liquid, covered, for 1 hour.

To make the sauce, remove the chicken from the liquid and strain. Mix the arrowroot with 1 tablespoon of water. Bring the liquid from the chicken to a boil again and add the arrowroot mixture. Cook, stirring, over high over high heat for 5 minutes or until thickened. Drizzle the sauce over the chicken and serve.

Zucchini Nut Loaf

Makes 3 loaves

4 ½   cups all-purpose flour

1   cup instant vanilla pudding mix

3   teaspoons cinnamon

1 ½   teaspoons ground nutmeg

1 ½   teaspoons baking soda

¾   teaspoon baking powder

½   teaspoon salt

3   cups finely shredded unpeeled zucchini

¾   teaspoon grated lemon peel

¾   cup vegetable oil

2 ½   cups sugar

3   eggs

1 ½   cups chopped walnuts

Grease and flour three 8 x 4-inch loaf pans. Preheat oven to 350°.

Sift together the flour, pudding mix, cinnamon, nutmeg, baking soda, baking powder, and salt in a large bowl.

In another bowl, with a mixer, beat together the oil, sugar, and eggs. Add the zucchini and lemon peel and mix well.

Gradually mix the dry ingredients into the zucchini mixture, stirring just intil blended. Do not overmix. Toss the walnuts with just enough flour to lightly coat them. (This will keep them from sinking to the bottom during baking.) Gently fold the nuts into the batter.

Scoop the batter into the prepared loaf pans and bake for 45–50 minutes or until done. Remove from oven, set on a wire rack, and allow to cool in the pans for 15 minutes. Remove loaves from the pans and finish cooling on the wire rack.

Double Ginger Blackberry Crisp

Serves 6

Filling

3 cups blackberries

3 tablespoons brown sugar

½ teaspoon cinnamon

1 teaspoon ground ginger

Topping

1 cup all-purpose flour

1 cup brown sugar

1 teaspoon baking powder

¼ teaspoon salt

¼ teaspoon allspice

½ teaspoon ground ginger

1 heaping tablespoon chopped crystallized ginger

2 eggs, beaten

½ cup (1 stick) butter, cut into small pieces

Preheat oven to 400°.

Combine the blackberries, brown sugar, cinnamon, and ginger and spoon into an 8-inch baking dish.

In a bowl, combine the flour, brown sugar, baking powder, salt, allspice, and ground and crystallized ginger. Blend in the eggs (the mixture will be crumbly).

Sprinkle the topping mixture over the filling and dot with the butter. Bake for 25–30 minutes or until the top is crispy and brown. Serve warm.

Blackberry Rhubarb Pie

Makes one 9-inch pie

2 ½   cups all-purpose flour

½   teaspoon salt

½   cup (1 stick) butter, chilled and cut into pieces (or ½ cup vegetable shortening)

5   tablespoons sugar

¼   cup ice water

3   cups peeled, sliced rhubarb

3   cups fresh blackberries

2   tablespoons lemon juice

¼   cup all-purpose flour

1 ¼   cup sugar

¼   teaspoon salt

¼   teaspoon ground nutmeg

¼   cup (½ stick) butter, chilled and cut into pieces

In a bowl, combine the flour and salt. With a pastry blender or fingers, cut the ½ cup of butter or shortening into the flour until the mixture resembles very coarse meal. Add the 5 tablespoons of sugar. Gradually add just enough ice water to form a ball. Separate into 2 balls, wrap in plastic wrap, and chill for 1 hour.

Roll one piece of the dough out on a lightly floured surface to about a ⅛-inch thickness and gently ease into a 9-inch pie pan. Roll out the remaining pastry for the top crust.

Preheat oven to 425°. Place the rhubarb and blackberries in a large bowl. Sprinkle with the lemon juice and toss to coat well. In a small bowl combine the flour, sugar, salt and nutmeg. Add to the fruit and stir.

Put the fruit mixture into the pastry-lined pie pan and dot with the ¼ cup of butter. Lay the top crust over the fruit, prick with a fork for venting, and trim and flute the edges.

Bake 25 minutes, then reduce the heat to 350° and bake until the juices are bubbling and the top is browned, about 25 minutes longer.

Plum Port-Wine and Maple Tart

Makes one 9-inch tart

Pastry

1 ¾ cups all-purpose flour

¼ cup slivered almonds

1 teaspoon cinnamon

¼ cup sugar

10 tablespoons (1 ¼ sticks) butter, slightly chilled and cut into pieces

1 egg

1 tablespoon milk

1 teaspoon lemon juice

1 teaspoon vanilla extract

1 tablespoon grated orange peel

Filling

9 ripe purple plums

½ cup plum jelly

½ cup cream

2 teaspoons sugar

1 cup port wine

FOR THE PASTRY: Put the almonds in the bowl of a food processor and pulse just until they are finely ground (not pasty). Add the butter, egg, milk, lemon juice, vanilla extract, and orange peel and pulse two or three times to blend.

Combine the flour, sugar, and cinnamon in a bowl. Add to the mixture in the food processor and pulse gently just until combined. (Do not overmix or the dough will be tough.) Wrap the dough and refrigerate for 30 minutes.

Preheat the oven to 350°. On a lightly floured surface roll the dough into a 12-inch round. Gently ease the dough into a 9-inch tart pan (the edges should extend about ½ inch above the sides). Line the shell with foil and place pie weights on the foil. Bake the shell about 30 minutes, until golden brown. Carefully remove the foil and weights and allow the shell to cool completely.

FOR THE FILLING: Wash the plums; cut them in half and remove the pits. In a saucepan, heat the port wine over medium heat. Add the plums and simmer about 15 minutes, or until they are tender but still retain their shape. Remove the plums from the wine and set aside.

To make a glaze, increase the heat to high and boil the liquid until it is reduced to about ¼ cup in volume. Reduce the heat to medium and add the plum jelly. Cook, stirring, for 2 minutes. Remove from heat and let cool.

Whip the cream and sugar together. (Note: It is always better to slightly under-whip cream, as it will have a nicer texture.) Brush the bottom of the cooled tart shell with the port wine and plum jelly glaze. Spread the whipped cream over the glaze, then arrange the plums skin-side up over the whipped cream. Brush the tops of the plums with the remaining glaze.

Blood Orange Vinaigrette

1   cup blood orange juice
¾   cup vegetable oil
1 ½   teaspoons red wine vinegar

In a small pan, boil the orange juice until it is reduced by half; let juice cool in refrigerator for 15 minutes. Place the reduced juice in a blender container. Set the blender to a low setting, and with the blender running, gradually add the red wine vinegar and vegetable oil.

The vinaigrette is delicious tossed with baby greens or any desired salad combination.

Cantaloupe Avocado Salsa

¼   cup finely diced cantaloupe
½   cup finely diced avocado
5   tablespoons minced red pepper
3   tablespoons minced green pepper
3   tablespoons lime juice
2   cloves garlic, minced
1   tablespoon chopped cilantro
      Juice of medium sized lemon

Combine all of the ingredients and let set for one hour. Serve with pan fried or grilled fish such as grouper, red snapper, orange roughy, or filet of sole.

August

is the month when people go somewhere else, anyplace but where they spend the majority of their time. Whether it is to the most sophisticated of places such as Paris, or to the simplest such as Putnam County, the collective urge to leave possesses them.

So off they go—trundling down the roads leading out of town, heavy with baggage—to the resorts, the beaches, the parks, out of state and overseas. Following everyone else, they entrust town, kitchen, and campus to the likes of those of us who feel that we can truly engage and enjoy our surroundings now that we have the place to ourselves. Consequently, August at the Inn is slow, a time when I often have the Walden kitchen to myself, to turn up the radio (classical music for preparation, blues for clean-up) and toy with new recipes, or revisit classic old recipes with many steps. These involve the creation of long simmering stocks, gelatinous velutes, mother sauces, demiglacés, glacés des viandes, and "made from scratch" bases. I can indulge every phase of the recipe, a sort of culinary tai chi where the process itself is enjoyed as much or more than the end result.

I have time to marvel again at the fact that cooking is an artistic discipline, where the completed whole is so much greater than its humble parts. The way, for instance, that onions, water, hard bread, and a little cheese—not really memorable in and of themselves—can combine to create the splendid, classic taste of a French onion soup.

I have time to walk the dreamy and deserted DePauw campus, to admire the ancient, branching crookedness of my favorite campus tree for as long as I want, without risking the bemused attention of passersby. I have time to remember that the best times can be had in places half forgotten. I have time to pack picnic boxes with crab cake sandwiches, black bean relish, and sparkling water laced with the essences of carrots, apples, and limes fresh from the juicer. I can bicycle out with my box lunch to a solitary country bridge perched like a peephole to eternity over a warm weed-wandering trickily stream. Many of those times described as "dog days" in the experience of others are indeed halcyon for temperaments like mine.

Lake Perch Poached in a Pocket

This is a wonderfully simple dish perfectly suited for outdoor summertime grilling.

Serves 4

1 ½   pounds lake perch
4   tablespoons butter or margarine
       Juice of 2 lemons
⅓   cup chardonnay
⅓   dry vermouth
2   teaspoons chopped fresh thyme (or 4 teaspoons fresh lemon grass)
1 ½   teaspoons Tabasco sauce
½   cup chopped mushrooms
½   cup chopped scallions
½   cup chopped tomatoes
1   cup small green grapes
1   tablespoon chopped fresh parsley
½   cup cream or evaporated skim milk
1   teaspoon lemon pepper

Cut four 10 x 10-inch squares of aluminum foil.

Divide the perch into 4 portions and place on the foil squares. Top each portion of fish with 1 tablespoon of butter or margarine. Combine the remaining ingredients and pour over the fish and butter. Gather the sides and corners of the foil squares together and crimp securely to seal.

Place the foil "pockets" on a hot grill and cook for 20 minutes.

Slide the contents of the foil pockets onto dinner plates and serve.

Pan-roasted Chicken and Mushrooms

Serves 4

½   cup balsamic vinegar

2 ½   tablespoons brown sugar

2 ½   teaspoons coarse kosher salt

1 ½   pounds (3–4 large) ripe yellow tomates

12   scallions, thinly sliced

5   serrano chilies, stemmed and quartered lengthwise

1   tablespoon black or yellow mustard seeds

1   tablespoon cumin seeds

2   teaspoons cracked black peppercorns

1 ½   teaspoons crushed red pepper flakes

½   teaspoon turmeric

1   piece fresh ginger (about 1 ½ inches long), peeled and julienned

3   garlic cloves, thinly sliced

½   cup olive oil

4   5-ounce boneless, skinless chicken breasts
     Salt and pepper

2   tablespoons vegetable oil

½   cup chardonnay

1   cup stemmed and quartered mushrooms

In a saucepan, combine the balsamic vinegar, brown sugar, and salt. Stir over medium heat until sugar is completely dissolved. Remove from heat.

Peel, seed, and chop the tomatoes. Combine with the scallions and peppers.

Measure the mustard seeds, cumin, black peppercorns, crushed red pepper, and turmeric on a plate, with the ginger and garlic. In a medium saucepan, heat the olive oil over high heat until almost smoking. Add the ingredients on the plate all at once and reduce heat to medium. Cook, stirring, for 1 minute. Remove from heat and add the vinegar mixture.

Pour the seasoned vinegar mixture over the tomatoes, scallions, and peppers and let cool. Cover with plastic wrap and refrigerate for at least 3 hours. (This relish keeps, refreigerated, up to 3 days.)

Preheat oven to 375°. Sprinkle the chicken with salt and pepper to taste. Heat the vegetable oil in an oven-proof skillet over high heat. Add the chicken and the mushrooms to the hot oil and sauté for 5 minutes. Turn the chicken and sauté for another 5 minutes.

Add the chardonnay to the chicken and mushrooms and continue cooking until the wine sizzles and begins to evaporate. Place the skillet in the oven for 15 minutes, or until the chicken is cooked through.

To serve, spoon some of the relish on serving plates and arrange the chicken and mushrooms on top.

Ginger Peach Bread

5 cups all-purpose flour
1 cup instant vanilla pudding mix
¾ teaspoon nutmeg
1 tablespoon ground ginger
1 tablespoon plus ½ teaspoon baking powder
1 teaspoon salt
1 cup (2 sticks) butter, softened
2 ½ cups sugar
1 teaspoon vanilla extract
5 eggs
1 ½ cups milk
2 cups diced peaches

Grease and flour three 8 x 4-inch loaf pans. Preheat oven to 350°.

In a large mixing bowl, sift together the flour, pudding mix, nutmeg, ginger, baking powder, and salt.

With a mixer, beat the butter and the sugar together until light and fluffy. Add eggs one at a time, beating well after each addition. Add the vanilla extract.

Alternately mix in the dry ingredients and the milk, stirring just enough to blend. Do not overmix. Fold in the peaches.

Scoop the batter into the prepared pans and bake for 40–45 minutes or until done. Remove the pans from oven, set on a wire rack, and allow to cool in the pans for 15 minutes. Remove the loaves from the pans and finish cooling on the wire rack.

Red Snapper Rings with Corn and Black Bean Relish

Serves 4

4	red snapper filets
1	quart vegetable or fish stock, or water
1/3	cup chopped red or sweet vidalia onion
1	tablespoon peanut oil
2	tablespoons balsamic vinegar
1	tablespoon chardonnay
1	tablespoon vermouth
1	tablespoon honey
2	teaspoons Dijon mustard
2	teaspoons Tabasco sauce
2	cloves garlic, minced
2	red peppers, roasted, peeled, seeded (see page 52)
1/4	cup sweet corn
1/4	cup cooked black beans
1	large apple, chopped (any variety that is not too tart or mealy)
	Fresh chives

FOR THE FISH: Preheat oven to 375°. Heat the broth or water to simmering. Roll the red snapper filets into rings, skin side out, and fasten with toothpicks. Place the fish rings on their sides in a 2-quart baking dish.

Pour the hot liquid over the fish and place in the oven for 15 minutes or just until the fish is opaque. (Note: If using a glass dish, place on a towel before pouring the hot liquid in, so the dish will not crack.) Carefully remove the fish to a platter and set aside, keeping warm. Pour the liquid into another pot and simmer briskly until it is reduced to about 1 cup in volume.

FOR THE RELISH: Over medium-high heat, sauté the onion in peanut oil for 5 minutes or until transluscent. Reduce heat to medium and add the vinegar, chardonnay, vermouth, honey, Dijon mustard, Tabasco sauce, and garlic and continue cooking for 5 minutes. Dice the peppers and add to the mixture, along with the sweet corn and black beans. Cook for another 5 minutes. Add the chopped apple and remove from heat.

To serve, spoon the relish into the red snapper rings and drizzle the remaining broth over them. Garnish with fresh chive strands across the middle of each snapper ring.

Corn, Cucumber, and Potato Chowder

Serves 4

½   cup diced red onion
1   tablespoon olive oil
1   cup sweet corn
1   tablespoon of fresh chopped sage (or 1 teaspoon of dried sage)
½   teaspoon curry powder
2   cloves garlic, minced
½   teaspoon nutmeg
1   cup potatoes, cooked, peeled, and diced
¾   cup chopped, peeled, and seeded cucumber
3 ½ cups vegetable or chicken broth, or water
     Salt and cayenne pepper
½   cup chopped scallions
½   cup crumbled goat cheese

In a large saucepan, sauté the onion in the olive oil for 5 minutes. Add corn and sauté for another 5 minutes. Add the sage, curry powder, garlic, nutmeg, potatoes, and cucumbers and continue to cook, stirring, for 2 more minutes.

Add the broth or water and season with salt and cayenne pepper to taste. Simmer for 15 minutes.

Remove from the heat and sprinkle in the chopped scallions. Ladle soup into bowls and crumble a little goat cheese on top. Dust with a little cayenne pepper and serve.

Pan-roasted Pork Chops with Peach Chutney

Serves 4

4   1-inch thick pork loin chops, trimmed of fat
1   cup milk
1 ½ cups cornmeal
3   tablespoons vegetable oil
     Peach Chutney (recipe follows)
     Fresh mint

Preheat oven to 350°. Dip the pork chops in milk and coat on both sides with cornmeal. Heat oil in an oven-proof skillet over high heat and lightly brown chops on both sides. Place in oven and bake uncovered for 25–30 minutes. Serve with a dollop of Peach Chutney and a sprig of fresh mint.

Peach Chutney

1   cinnamon stick, broken
8   whole cloves
⅓   teaspoon coriander seeds
12   medium peaches, peeled, pitted, and diced
2   cups sugar
1 ½ cups cider vinegar
1   tablespoon chopped candied lemon peel
1   teaspoon finely minced fresh ginger

Place the cinnamon stick, cloves, and coriander seeds together on a square of several thicknesses of cheesecloth. Gather the cheesecloth and tie, encasing the spices, to form a bag.

Combine the sugar, vinegar, lemon peel, and ginger in a large saucepan and bring to a one-bubble boil. Add the spice bag and peaches, reduce the heat, and simmer 5 minutes, stirring occasionally. Remove and discard spice bag and serve.

Zucchini and Chive Tartlets

Pastry

- 1 ¼ cups all-purpose flour
- ¼ teaspoon salt
- ½ cup (1 stick) butter, well chilled and cut into pieces
- 1 egg yolk, lightly beaten
- 2 teaspoons ice water

Filling

- 3 medium zucchini
- 1 tablespoon olive oil
- ½ cup chopped scallions
- 2 cloves garlic, minced
- 2 teaspoons chopped fresh dill
- ½ cup buttermilk
- 2 small eggs, beaten
- 3 tablespoons coarse-grain Dijon mustard
- Salt and pepper
- ¼ cup grated Gruyère cheese

FOR THE PASTRY: Sift the flour and the salt together. With a knife, cut the butter into the flour until mixture resembles coarse meal. Lightly work in the egg yolk and the chilled water to form a soft dough. Cover with plastic wrap and refrigerate for 30 minutes.

Preheat oven to 375°. Divide dough into 8 pieces and roll each piece into a 4 ½-inch circle. Line 4-inch tartlet tins with the dough and chill for 10 minutes. Line the pastry shells with foil and cover place pie weights on the foil. Bake 25 minutes or until golden. Carefully remove the weights and the foil.

FOR THE FILLING: Cook the zucchini in simmering water for 10 to 15 minutes or just until tender. Cut into thin (⅛-inch) slices and set aside.

Sauté the scallions, garlic, and dill in the oil over moderate heat for 5 minutes. Divide the mixture among the tartlets and arrange the zucchini slices on top.

Mix the buttermilk, eggs, and mustard, and add salt and pepper to taste. Pour the mixture over the zucchini and sprinkle with Gruyère cheese. Bake for at 375° for 20 to 25 minutes or until golden brown.

Black Bean and Tomato Wild Rice

Serves 4

2	tablespoons olive oil
¾	cup chopped mushrooms
3	whole tomatoes, chopped
1	tablespoon chopped sun-dried tomatoes
1 ½	cup cooked wild rice or wild rice blend (see below)
¾	cup cooked black beans
	Salt and pepper
¾	cup chopped scallions

In a heavy saucepan, heat the oil over moderate heat. Add the mushrooms and sauté for 5 minutes. Add both kinds of tomatoes and sauté for 2 minutes more.

Add the rice and black beans and cook for 5 minutes. Salt and pepper to taste. Add the chopped scallions just before serving.

Basic Wild Rice

Not actually "rice," wild rice is the edible grain of a tall aquatic North American perennial grass. It doesn't absorb the cooking liquid the same way as regular rice, and it takes longer to cook.

3	cups vegetable broth
1	cup wild rice, rinsed and drained
1	teaspoon minced garlic
1	tablespoon chopped fresh oregano
2	teaspoons fresh chopped thyme
1	bay leaf

In a medium saucepan, bring the vegetable broth to a boil. Add the wild rice and the rest of the ingredients and return to a boil over medium heat.

Reduce heat to low, cover, and cook until the wild rice is tender, about 40 minutes. Drain any excess liquid and discard the bay leaf and serve.

Soft-Shell Crabs over Wild Rice

At certain times of the year, the crabs molt and are left with just a thin coating, or "soft" shell, which is edible.

Serves 4

8   soft-shell crabs, cleaned*
1   cup wild rice or wild rice blend
¼   cup chopped sun-dried tomatoes
¼   cup pecans
1   each red and yellow peppers, roasted, peeled, and seeded (see page 52)
¾   cup peeled and julienned jicama
½   medium red onion, finely sliced
2   teaspoon sesame seeds

Preheat oven to 350°. Rub crabs with a little olive oil and spread on a baking sheet and bake for 15 minutes.

Cook the rice according to the method on page 88. Mix in the chopped dried tomatoes and the pecans.

Slice the peppers into thin strips. Add the jicama and red onion. Sauté the vegetables in a tablespoon of olive oil over high heat for 3 minutes. Season with salt and pepper to taste. Sprinkle with the sesame seeds.

To serve, place the crabs over the rice mixture and surround with a ring of the vegetables.

If using fresh crabs, have the fish market clean them for you.

Spiced Applesauce Tart

Makes one 9-inch tart

Crust

3	cups crushed gingersnaps
½	cup melted butter

Topping

¼	cup butter, softened
½	cup firmly packed brown sugar
¾	cup rolled oats
⅓	cup all-purpose flour
½	cup coarsely chopped pecans
¼	teaspoon salt

Filling

4	Granny Smith apples (or other suitable baking apple), peeled, cored and cut into small pieces
¼	cup water
½	cup sugar
2	eggs
¾	cup heavy cream
½	teaspoon cinnamon
¼	cup (½ stick) butter, melted
¼	teaspoon salt
1	teaspoon ground cloves
½	teaspoon allspice

Combine the crushed gingersnaps and melted butter and press into a 9-inch tart pan.

Mix the topping ingredients until the mixture is crumbly. Set aside.

In a saucepan, bring the apples and water to a simmer and cover and cook over moderate heat, stirring and mashing occasionally, until thickened, 20–30 minutes. (A few small lumps are okay.) Remove from heat and let cool for 10 minutes. Stir in remaining filling ingredients.

Preheat oven to 375°. Pour the filling into the gingersnap crust and sprinkle with the topping. Bake for 25 minutes, until topping is very crispy and brown.

September's

shameless sunsets smear lipstick on the warm teal blue collar of the sky with the ardor of a departing lover. The young Autumn's tender spirit draws us after work to the sidewalk bistros and outdoor porches and portals, to the comfort of conversation and good food. I think of Beaujolais-scented game hen, roast duckling with green peppercorn and apricot sauce, shrimp and squash bisque, or maybe just a good cup of cappuccino with a raspberry-almond cookie and a great book of short stories.

Heartland Summer Harvest Tart

Serves 8

Tart shell

1 ¼   cups all-purpose flour
¼   cup cake flour
1 ½   tablespoons sugar
¾   cup (1 ½ sticks) butter, chilled and cut into small pieces
1 ½   tablespoons cream
1   egg, beaten
1   tablespoon grated lemon peel
1   teaspoon vanilla extract

Lemon filling

1   cup sugar
½   cup lemon juice
½   cup (1 stick) butter
3   tablespoons grated lemon peel
3   eggs, beaten
1   cup fresh raspberries
1   cup fresh blackberries

FOR SHELL: Combine the egg, cream and vanilla extract. In another bowl, using a pastry blender or your fingers, combine the flour, sugar, lemon peel, and butter until it resembles coarse meal. (This may be done with a food processor or electric mixture. Be careful to use low speed and do not overprocess.) Add the egg, cream, and vanilla mixture and blend just until mixture forms a ball. Wrap in plastic and refrigerate 30 minutes.

Preheat oven to 350°. Roll the dough on a lightly floured surface to about a 12-inch diameter circle and ease into a 9-inch tart pan. (The edges of the dough should extend a bit beyond the edges of the pan to allow for shrinkage while baking.) Line crust with foil and cover with pie weights and bake crust 20 minutes. Remove the foil and weights and bake another 10 minutes, or until lightly browned. Remove from oven and let cool.

FOR FILLING: Whisk eggs in a medium bowl. Combine sugar, lemon juice, lemon peel, and butter in a heavy saucepan and bring just to boiling (a one-bubble boil). Gradually add the mixture to the beaten eggs, whisking constantly so eggs are incorporated smoothly. Return mixture to the saucepan and cook over low heat, whisking constantly, for about 20 minutes or until mixture becomes thick enough to run in a slow ribbon off the back of a spoon. Remove from heat and let cool.

Spoon the filling into the tart shell and arrange the berries on top in alternating concentric circles.

Note: This filling is best when made one day in advance. Refrigerate until ready to use.

Pan-roasted Eggplant and Garlic Soup

Serves 6

1 ½	leeks
2	tablespoons peanut oil
2	cups chicken or vegetable broth or water
3	Idaho potatoes, peeled and cut into 1-inch pieces
1	teaspoon salt
½	teaspoon pepper
1	medium eggplant, peeled and cut into ½-inch pieces
10	garlic cloves, unpeeled
3	tablespoons corn oil
1	cup milk (whole or skim)
¼	cup finely chopped basil

Cut the leeks in half lengthwise, clean, and cut into ½-inch pieces. In a large saucepan, sauté the leek in the peanut oil over medium-high heat for 5 minutes. Add the broth, potatoes, salt, and pepper. Bring just to a boil, and reduce the heat to low. Cover and simmer until the vegetables are tender, about 20 minutes.

Preheat oven to 350°. In a medium bowl, toss the eggplant and the unpeeled garlic cloves in the corn oil, spread on a baking sheet, and roast in the oven for 20 minutes. Remove from the oven and peel and mince the garlic cloves.

Strain the leek and potatoes from the soup and purée in a food processor with the eggplant and a little of the cooking liquid. Return the puréed vegetables to the pan and add the garlic, stir in the milk and bring just to a simmer over medium-high heat. Add the chopped basil and serve.

Indiana Sweet Corn and Red Pepper Tart

This state, where corn and children grow tall overnight, now has as much claim as the land of my birth on my emotional roots. With time they have grown deep into the subsoil of Hoosier culture and life—deep enough to find secrets not obvious to those just passing through. This handsome heartland can bestow gifts of strength, confidence, and self-esteem on those who combine energy to claim them, with faith in its ability to do so.

Pastry Shell

1 ½ cups all purpose flour
2 tablespoons sugar
⅛ teaspoon salt
1 teaspoon baking powder
½ cup (1 stick) butter, chilled and cut into small pieces
¼ cup (2 ounces) cream cheese
1 egg yolk
1 ½ teaspoons vanilla
1 teaspoon lemon juice

Filling

1 cup heavy cream or evaporated skim milk
2 medium eggs
¼ cup honey or maple syrup
1 teaspoon nutmeg
1 teaspoon ginger
½ teaspoon each salt and pepper
2 cups fresh sweet corn
1 medium red pepper, seeded and diced

FOR PASTRY SHELL: In a large bowl combine the flour, sugar, salt, and baking powder. Add the butter and cream cheese, working into the flour mixture using fingertips or pastry blender. The mixture should be very coarse, with pieces the size of small peas.

Make a well in the center and add the egg yolk, vanilla, and lemon juice. Using fingers or fork gently stir until the mixture forms a soft ball. Cover and refrigerate for 15 minutes.

On a lightly floured surface, roll the dough into about an 11–12-inch circle.

Gently ease the dough into a 9-inch tart pan. (The edges of the dough should extend slightly above the rim of the pan.)

FOR FILLING: Warm the cream or milk just to the point of boiling.

Beat eggs, maple sugar or honey, spices, and salt and pepper together with a whisk in a large bowl. Pour half the hot milk into the bowl, whisking constantly. Pour egg mixture back into the saucepan with the remainder of the milk, whisking constantly. Continue to whisk and cook over medium heat for about 10 minutes until mixture thickens and becomes a smooth custard.

Add the sweet corn and diced pepper to the custard and pour the mixture into the prepared pastry shell. Bake at 350° for 35 minutes or until knife inserted near center comes out clean.

Red Bean, Corn, and Red Pepper Chowder

Serves 4

⅓   cup diced onion
1   tablespoon olive oil
½   cup chopped portabella mushrooms
½   cup chardonnay
¾   cup cooked red beans (may use canned)
¾   cup sweet corn (fresh or frozen)
3   tomatillos, husked and chopped
1   tablespoon chili-garlic paste*
4   red peppers, roasted, peeled, and seeded (see page 52)
4   cups broth or water
⅓   cup chopped scallion

Sauté the onion in the olive oil over medium-high heat for 5 minutes or until onion is transluscent. Add the mushrooms and chardonnay and continue to cook until liquid is reduced by half. Reduce heat to medium and add the red beans, sweet corn, tomatillos, and chili-garlic paste.

Purée peppers in a blender and add to the other ingredients in the pan. Add broth and simmer for 15 minutes, stirring occasionally. Add scallions and serve immediately.

Available at specialty or Oriental food stores.

Bruce's Upside-down Pear Skillet Cake

Serves 8–10

1   cup brown sugar

⅓   cup (1 stick butter) cut into small pieces

1 ⅓   cups all-purpose flour

1 ⅓   cups sugar

2   teaspoons cinnamon

1 ¼   teaspoons baking soda

½   teaspoon salt

2   eggs, beaten

½   cup vegetable oil

7   pears, peeled and cored

Preheat oven to 350°.

Combine the butter and brown sugar in a 12-inch cast iron skillet, spreading to cover the entire surface. Place in the oven for 5 minutes, or until butter is melted. Remove from the oven and whisk until the sugar dissolves.

Finely grate 2 of the pears, and slice the other 5 pears into six wedges each.

In a bowl, mix flour, cinnamon, sugar, baking soda, and salt. Add the eggs and grated pear and blend well.

Arrange the pear wedges close together in the skillet in the butter and sugar. Pour the batter evenly over the pears. Bake one hour until springy. Cool for twenty minutes and turn out, upside down, on a platter. Serve warm with whipped cream.

Fresh Fruit with Champagne Sabayon (page 72).

Dolly Mount Crab Cakes (page 109) accompanied by Black Bean and Tomato Wild Rice (page 88).

Wild Rice with Macadamia Nuts and Dried Cranberries

Serves 6

3	cups Vegetable Broth (recipe follows)
1	cup wild rice, rinsed and drained
1	teaspoon minced garlic
1	tablespoon chopped fresh oregano
2	teaspoons chopped fresh thyme
1	bay leaf
¼	cup macadamia nuts
½	cup dried cranberries
¼	cup finely chopped celery
	Salt and pepper

In a medium saucepan, bring the broth to a boil. Add the wild rice, garlic, oregano, thyme, and bay leaf and return to a boil. Cover the pan and place in a preheated 350° oven for about 40 minutes, or until the rice is tender.

Discard the bay leaf. Stir in the macadamia nuts, cranberries, and celery. Season with salt and pepper to taste.

Vegetable Broth

Makes about a half gallon

1 ½	leeks, cleaned and coarsely chopped (see page 27)
3	medium carrots, coarsely chopped
4	celery ribs, coarsely chopped
6	sprigs fresh oregano
6	sprigs fresh thyme
1	bay leaf
1 ½	teaspoons whole peppercorns

Combine all ingredients in a stockpot with 12 cups of water and bring to a boil over high heat. Reduce heat to low and simmer for 1 hour. Strain the broth and let cool. Keeps up to 3 days refrigerated.

Walnut Shortcakes with Blueberries and Pears

Shortcakes

- 3/4 cup walnut pieces
- 1/2 cup granulated sugar
- 1 tablespoon brown sugar
- 2 cups cake flour
- 1/2 teaspoon salt
- 1 tablespoon baking powder
- 1/2 cup (1 stick) butter, chilled and cut into small pieces
- 1/2 cup heavy cream

Blueberry-Pear Topping

- 1 pear, peeled, cored, and sliced
- 1 cup blueberries
- 1/2 cup sugar
- 1 teaspoon pear liqueur
- 3 tablespoons butter
- 1/4 cup brown sugar
- Whipped cream

FOR SHORTCAKES: Spread the walnut pieces on a baking sheet and toast in a 375° oven for 5 minutes. Let cool slightly and place in the bowl of a food processor with the granulated sugar. Pulse just until the nuts are coarsely ground.

In a medium bowl, combine the walnut mixture, brown sugar, flour, salt, baking powder, and butter. With a pastry blender or your fingers, blend the ingredients until the mixture resembles very coarse meal. Slowly add the cream and mix just until the mixture forms a soft mass.

On a lightly floured surface, roll or pat the dough to about 1 inch thick and cut into six 2 1/2-inch-wide circles. Reduce the oven heat to 350°. Place the circles on a baking tray and bake until golden brown, about 35 minutes.

FOR THE TOPPING: Combine the pears, blueberries, sugar, and liqueur in a large saucepan. Cook over medium heat, stirring, until the sugar is dissolved. Add the butter and cook until the mixture thickens slightly, 1–2 minutes.

To serve, split the shortcake biscuits and place the bottoms on dessert plates and cover with some whipped cream and the topping. Top with the second half of the shortcakes and serve with a dollop of whipped cream on the side.

Note: The shortcakes and topping are best when fresh. Bake the shortcakes the day you plan to serve them and prepare the blueberry-pear topping immediately before serving.

Grilled Chicken with Fruit and Honey Sauce

This is excellent with rice and steamed fresh summer vegetables.

Serves 4

1	cup orange juice
1	cup pineapple juice
1	cup peach juice
¼	cup vegetable oil
½	cup fresh tarragon
¼	cup fresh basil
¾	cup honey
½	cup Grand Marnier
4	chicken breasts, boneless and skinless
	Salt and pepper

Combine juices in a saucepan. Bring to a boil and reduce to ⅓ the original volume. Remove from heat.

In another small pan warm the honey, oil, basil, and tarragon over low heat. Add to the reduced juices and add the Grand Marnier. Reserve ⅓ cup of sauce for basting the chicken.

Rub the chicken with a little vegetable oil and season with salt and pepper to taste. Grill 10 minutes per side or until done, basting occasionally with the sauce.

Spread a small pool of the sauce on 4 dinner plates. Place the chicken in the pool of sauce and serve.

Pistachio Encrusted Scallops with Lime Butter

Serves 4

1 ½	cups shelled pistachios
1 ½	cup bread crumbs
1	pound fresh bay scallops
½	cup flour
¾	cup milk
⅓	cup olive oil
1	cup (2 sticks) unsalted butter
	Juice of 4 limes
½	cup chardonnay
½	cup heavy cream
	Fresh basil leaves

Spread the pistachios on a baking sheet and toast in a 375° oven for 5 minutes. Let cool and place in the bowl of a food processor. Pulse once or twice, just enough to crush (do not overprocess) and combine with the bread crumbs.

Pat the scallops dry and dust lightly with flour. Dip in milk and coat with the pistachio-bread crumb mixture.

Preheat oven to 375°. In an oven-proof skillet heat the olive oil over moderate heat and sauté the scallops for 5 minutes. Place the scallops in the oven for 8 minutes.

Preheat a saucepan over medium-high heat. Add the butter and lime juice. Whisk briskly as the butter melts to thoroughly blend with the lime juice. Add the chardonnay and heavy cream and continue cooking, whisking constantly, for another 3 minutes.

Serve the sautéed scallops on a pool of the sauce and garnish with fresh basil leaves.

Goat Cheese Tart

Serves 4

1 ¼ cups all-purpose flour
½ cup (one stick) butter, chilled and cut into small pieces
¼ cup (2 ounces) cream cheese, softened
1 egg
2 teaspoons lemon juice
10 ounces goat cheese, crumbled
½ cup chopped scallions
½ cup chopped roasted, peeled, and seeded red pepper (see page 52)
2 teaspoons minced garlic
1 teaspoon chopped fresh thyme
1 tablespoon chopped fresh basil
1 tablespoon chopped fresh parsley
¼ cup chopped sun-dried tomatoes
4 eggs
1 cup cream or evaporated skim milk
½ cup buttermilk

Cut the butter and the cream cheese into small pieces and blend gently with the flour until it is crumbly, resembling coarse meal.

Make a well in the flour mixture and add the egg. Blend gently, adding the lemon juice just until the dough forms a soft mass. (Do not to overwork.) Wrap in plastic wrap and refrigerate for 15 minutes.

Preheat oven to 375°. Roll the dough out on a lightly floured surface to a 10 to 11-inch circle about ⅛-inch thick. Gently ease the dough into a 9-inch tart or pie pan (it should slightly extend beyond the edges of the pan). Line the dough with foil and top with pie weights and bake for 15 minutes. Carefully remove the foil and weights.

Reduce the oven heat to 350°. Sprinkle half of the goat cheese in the baked tart shell. Combine the scallions, red pepper, garlic, thyme, basil, parsley, and tomatoes and sprinkle over the goat cheese.

Blend the eggs, cream, and buttermilk together and pour over the top. Sprinkle with the remainder of the cheese and bake for 30 minutes or until set.

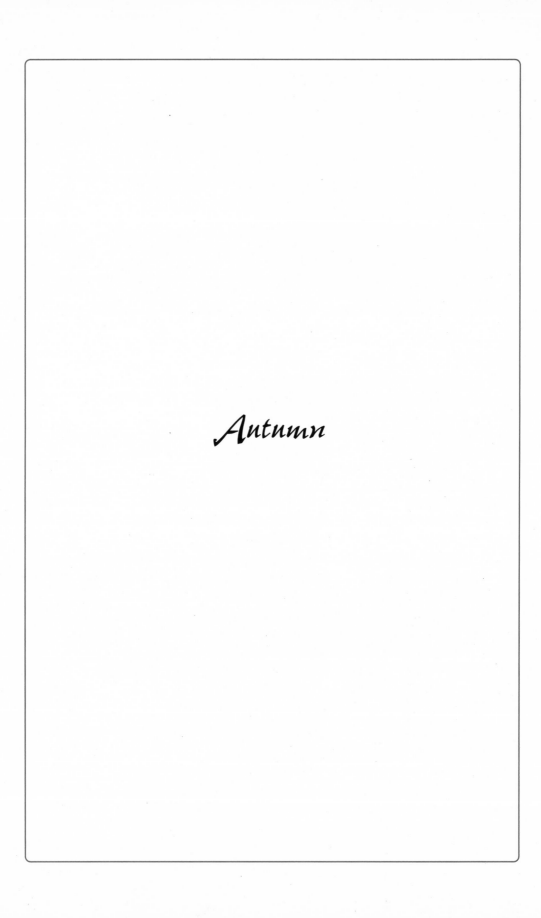

Autumn

October,

emerges from the cocoon of Summer's nurturing heat, with every sweet sun-wrinkled grain of goodness harvested and stored as the year begins its grand finale. Each tree in the open quad behind the Inn stands like a mythical king, regal in a lamplit cape of rustic foliage, casting leaves like coins in the basin of Autumn's fountain. We take a break from the work in the kitchen, sitting outside the back door on milk crates, feeling small beside this display of nature's sorcery, witnessing the magic in every turning leaf.

In October Farmer Max returns with a pickup truck full of deliriously colored pumpkins, squash, and sweet potatoes to decorate the plates and the lobby—his last delivery of the year. The largest pumpkin will have the word "Walden" scarred in its tough skin. Max learned this trick years ago, predicting in his own uncanny way which pumpkin was likely to grow largest and then carving the letters into the growing globe. Along with many other multicolored autumn gems it will decorate the lobby of the Walden.

The kitchen at the Inn bristles with activity, leaving us little time to contemplate the beauty of October—a beauty haunted by an unsettling power, like someone stole the secret tapestry of a departed, beloved soul and stretched it across the countryside to break another heart.

Cornish Hens with Warm Tomato and Herb Vinaigrette

Serves 2

2	Cornish hens
1	tablespoon olive oil
2	teaspoons minced garlic
	Salt and pepper
2	tomatoes, peeled, seeded, and chopped
½	tablespoon chopped sun-dried tomatoes
⅓	cup olive oil
⅓	cup chardonnay
⅓	cup balsmic vinegar
2	teaspoons chives
2	teaspoons cilantro
2	teaspoons chopped fresh parsley
2	teaspoons minced garlic
2	teaspoons Dijon mustard
2	teaspoons chopped fresh tarragon

Preheat oven to 350°. Rub the Cornish hens with the 1 tablespoon of olive oil and 2 teaspoons of minced garlic, and season with salt and pepper to taste. Roast for 40 minutes or until done. (Hens are done when juices run clear when pierced at thigh.)

Combine the fresh and dried tomatoes, olive oil, chardonnay, and balsamic vinegar in a saucepan and heat just to boiling. Reduce heat to medium and add the rest of the ingredients; simmer for 5 minutes, stirring constantly. Spoon over the Cornish hens and serve.

The building of the gingerbread house has become . . .
each year's last loving ritual . . .

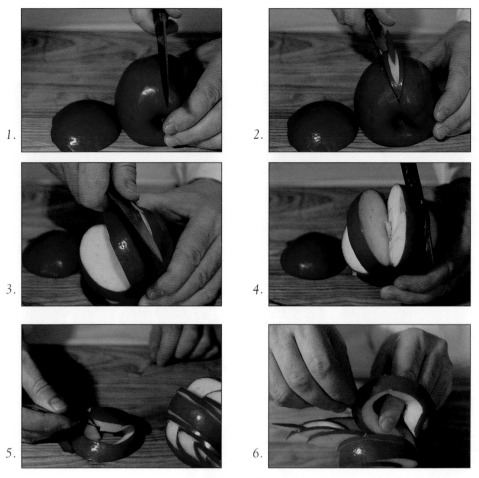

Apple Swan

One of my favorite garnishes—beautiful, yet easy to make: 1.) Cut a slice from one side of an apple to form a base; reserve the slice. 2.) With the apple cut-side down, cut a small v-shaped notch in the top center. 3–4.) Continue cutting even, v-shaped slices, almost to the core. Repeat the process on both sides of the apple. Fan the v-shaped slices in the notches to form the back and wings of the swan. 5.) From the first reserved slice, cut a curved piece with an inverted teardrop shape at the end to form the head and neck. Cut a small notch in the "teardrop" for the eye. 6.) Place the neck in the center notch of the apple.

Chef Vernon's Roasted Red Pepper Remoulade

This is featured with the Pecan and Herb-encrusted Halibut found on page 18, but is excellent with any broiled or grilled fish or chicken.

4	red peppers, roasted, peeled, and seeded (see page 52)
2 ½	tablespoons Dijon mustard
1	tablespoon capers
½	teaspoon minced garlic
1	teaspoon Worcestershire sauce
3	tablespoons sweet pickle relish
2	teaspoons Tabasco sauce

Combine all ingredients in the bowl of a food processor, and purée until the mixture is smooth.

Champagne and Vanilla Yogurt Sauce

This goes well with shrimp and lobster.

1	vanilla bean
2	cups plain yogurt
¾	cup champagne
1	tablespoon honey

Split the vanilla bean and scrape the seeds out. In a mixing bowl, stir the seeds and the split bean into the yogurt and refrigerate overnight.

Remove the vanilla bean and discard. Fold the honey and champagne into the yogurt and serve.

Almond, Apricot, and Dried Cranberry Tart

Serves 8

2 ¼   cups almonds

2 ¾   cups sifted cake flour

1   cup (2 sticks) plus 2 tablespoons butter, softened

1   cup sugar

5   eggs

½   teaspoon almond extract

4   medium-size apricots

½   cup dried cranberries

2   tablespoons butter

⅔   cup pure maple syrup

½   cup heavy cream

1   tablespoon lemon juice

2   tablespoons kirsch

½   teaspoon cinnamon

¼   teaspoon ground ginger

½   teaspoon nutmeg

Spread the almonds on a baking sheet and toast in a 375° oven for 5 minutes.

With a mixer, beat 1 cup of the butter and the sugar until light and fluffy. Add 2 eggs and almond extract.

Chop ¾ cup of the toasted almonds and blend with the flour. Add to the butter and egg mixture and mix just until mixture forms a soft mass (do not overmix). Wrap in plastic wrap and chill for 1 hour.

Roll the crust out on a lightly floured surface to about a 10-inch round. Lightly coat a 9-inch tart pan with vegetable oil. Ease the pastry into the pan and fit the edges to the top of the pan.

Place the rest of the almonds in the bowl of a food processor and pulse just until they are coarsely ground. Peel the apricots, remove the pits, and slice thinly. Melt 2 tablespoons of butter in a skillet and sauté the apricots and dried cranberries over medium-high heat, about 10 minutes.

In a large mixing bowl, whisk the remaining eggs with the syrup and cream. Add the kirsch, cinnamon, ginger, nutmeg, and almonds and continue to whisk for another 2 minutes. The mixture should be very light and fluffy.

Preheat oven to 350°. Spoon the apricots and cranberries into the prepared crust. Pour the egg and cream mixture over the fruit and bake for 50 minutes.

Roast Pork Loin with Creamed Apple Horseradish

Serves 4

1 ½   pound boneless pork loin
3   teaspoons minced garlic
1   tablespoon coarse-grain Dijon mustard
2   tablespoons olive oil
   Salt and cracked pepper
½   cup prepared horseradish (not cream-style)
½   cup sour cream
½   cup applesauce

Rub the pork loin with 1 tablespoon of the olive oil and the mustard and garlic. Season with salt and cracked pepper to taste.

Preheat oven to 375°. Heat the remaining olive oil in an oven-proof skillet and sear the meat on all sides. Place in the oven for 40 minutes or until an internal temperature of 155° is reached.

Combine the horseradish, sour cream, and applesauce. Serve on the side with the pork loin.

Gorgonzola and Roasted Vegetable Terrine

Serves 8–10

2	eggplants, peeled
2	large zucchini
3	large yellow squash
12	plum tomatoes, cored and halved
¾	cup olive oil
1 ½	cup crumbled gorgonzola cheese
3	eggs, beaten
2	cloves garlic, minced
2	teaspoons chopped fresh rosemary
	Salt and pepper

Cut the eggplant, zucchini, and yellow squash lengthwise into very thin slices (no more than ¼ inch thick). Spread the slices and the tomatoes on a baking sheet and brush lightly with olive oil (do in batches if necessary, so slices will not be stacked). Sprinkle lightly with salt and pepper. Place in preheated 400° oven and roast for 10 minutes. Remove from oven and let cool.

In a small bowl combine gorgonzola, eggs, garlic, rosemary, and 1 teaspoon each of salt and pepper.

Arrange the eggplant slices along the bottom and sides of a 9 x 5 x 3-inch glass or ceramic terrine dish so that the slices extend about 2 inches beyond the rim of the dish all around. Layer ⅓ of the zucchini slices lengthwise over the eggplant, then ⅓ of the yellow squash. Using a spatula, evenly spread ⅓ of the cheese mixture over the squash, and add a layer of the tomatoes over the cheese. Repeat the process until all ingredients are used. Fold in the overhanging eggplant slices to seal the terrine.

Preheat oven to 325°. Cover the terrine (use parchment paper if your dish doesn't have a cover) and place in a larger baking dish. Pour very hot (not boiling) water in the baking dish to about half-way up the sides of the terrine. Bake for 45 minutes; remove from the water bath and let cool to room temperature.

Cut a piece of sturdy cardboard to fit the top of the terrine and wrap in foil. Lightly cover the terrine with plastic wrap and place the cardboard on top. Weight the terrine by placing 2 or 3 cans (1-pound cans of tomatoes, for example) on top of the cardboard. Refrigerate overnight.

To serve, remove the weights and covering. Invert the terrine and unmold.

Cut into ¾-inch-thick slices, wiping the knife between cuts.

Dolly Mount Crab Cakes

Serves 4

½	cup lump crab meat
2	teaspoons olive oil
2	level tablespoons onions, minced
2	heaping tablespoons finely diced celery
1	clove garlic, minced
2	tablespoons chardonnay
1	tablespoon dry English mustard
½	red pepper, roasted, peeled, seeded, and diced (page 52)
¼	cup mayonnaise
2	tablespoons crushed water crackers
1	teaspoon Tabasco sauce
1	teaspoon salt
1	cup seasoned bread crumbs
	Vegetable oil
2	tablespoons mayonnaise
1	teaspoon Dijon mustard
1	teaspoon Worcestershire sauce

Spread the crabmeat on a shallow pan. Broil at 500° for 5 minutes or until the shell pieces turn white. Pick out any shell pieces and cartilage and discard.

In a skillet, heat the olive oil over medium-high heat and lightly sauté the onions, celery, and garlic. Add the chardonnay and continue cooking until the liquid evaporates. Add the dry mustard and remove from heat.

Stir the onions, celery, and garlic into the crabmeat. Add the diced red pepper, ¼ cup mayonnaise, crushed crackers, Tabasco sauce, and salt.

Shape the mixture into small patties, between ¼ and ½-inch thick and 2 inches in diameter. Coat with seasoned bread crumbs and sauté in vegetable oil over medium heat until brown, about 8 minutes per side. Combine the last three ingredients and serve on the side with the crab cakes.

Spinach, Basil, and Brie Turnovers

Serves 4

1	cup all-purpose flour
¼	teaspoon salt
¼	cup (½ stick) butter, chilled and cut into pieces
1	egg, beaten
2	teaspoons cold water
1	tablespoon olive oil
3	cups torn fresh spinach leaves
½	teaspoon nutmeg
1	teaspoon crushed garlic
	Salt and pepper
1	wheel of Brie
1	tablespoon pine nuts
1	tablespoon chopped sun-dried tomatoes
¼	cup fresh basil leaves

Combine the flour and ¼ teaspoon of salt. With a pastry blender or fingers, work the butter into the flour until it resembles very coarse meal.

Make a well and add the egg, working it gently into the flour and butter. Add water a very small bit at a time, just until the dough forms a mass. Wrap in plastic wrap and refrigerate for 15–30 minutes.

Preheat oven to 350°. Roll the dough to a ⅛-inch thickness and with a cookie or biscuit cutter cut dough into 2 ½-inch circles.

Heat the olive oil over medium heat and lightly sauté the spinach. Add the nutmeg, garlic, and salt and pepper to taste. Cut the Brie into grape-sized pieces.

Place a bit of spinach in each dough circle and top with a piece of Brie, the pine nuts, dried tomatoes, and a leaf of basil. Fold the circles over to form half-moon shapes, crimp the edges with a fork to seal and lightly pierce the tops with the fork to allow steam to vent. Bake for 20 minutes or until golden brown.

Corn and Red Pepper Pancakes

Something different to serve with chicken, fish, or a green salad.

Serves 4

1	cup cornmeal
¾	cup cake flour
2	teaspoons baking powder
½	teaspoon baking soda
1	teaspoon salt
½	teaspoon pepper
½	cup buttermilk
2	eggs, lightly beaten
¼	cup sweet corn (fresh or frozen)
2	red peppers, roasted, peeled, and seeded (see page 52)

Dice the red pepper. In a bowl, blend the cornmeal, cake flour, baking powder, baking soda, salt, and pepper.

Combine the eggs and buttermilk and add to the dry ingredients, blending just until smooth (do not overmix). Fold in the corn and red peppers.

Preheat a lightly oiled skillet or griddle over medium heat until it is hot. Drop the pancake mixture by spoonfuls into the hot skillet and brown on both sides. Serve hot.

November

consolidates the spirit. It rolls up the excesses and passions of the preceding months and stores them harmlessly on the hillside of the year's history like hay. A similar change becomes evident in our own moods and the foods we eat. Like a wedge of migrating birds pointed at the sunset, we gravitate to the safe and simple comforts we carry in our memories of home.

The collective expression of our impulse is the Thanksgiving holiday, when we seek to anchor the spirit in a familiar place. We give thanks for the successes we have achieved, and take a brief respite from the pursuit of those dreams that still manage to elude us.

America's tastes are uncharacteristically homogenous in November. Even immigrants like myself are drawn to the message and simple traditional fare of Thanksgiving. As a chef I try not to tinker too much with recipes that have been handed down like cultural heirlooms. Like everyone else, I simply concentrate on cooking the perfect turkey, the most savory dressing, and the best egg noodles I can make.

Oysters Walden

Serves 4

½   cup (1 stick) butter or margarine
    Juice of 1 lemon
1   cup chardonnay
16 mushroom caps, chopped
¾   cup cooked spinach
2   teaspoons minced garlic
2   teaspoons nutmeg
2   tablespoons chopped fresh oregano
4   tablespoons chopped fresh scallions
3   large tomatoes, chopped
1   tablespoon chopped sun-dried tomatoes
24 fresh oysters
1   cup sour cream
½   cup prepared horseradish
½   cup grated Parmesan cheese
½   cup shredded mozzarella cheese

Preheat a medium-size saucepan or skillet over high heat. Add the butter and when it sizzles add the lemon juice. Add mushrooms and sauté for 5 minutes. Add the chardonnay and continue to cook over high heat until the wine is nearly evaporated.

Add the spinach, garlic, nutmeg, oregano, scallions, and fresh and dried tomatoes. Sauté for 5 more minutes and remove from heat.

Shuck the oysters, reserving 24 half-shells. (The oysters can be shucked by the market where purchased, if desired.) Distribute the mushroom and spinach mixture among the reserved half-shells and top with the the oysters.

Combine the sour cream and horseradish and spread on top of the oysters. Sprinkle with Parmesan and mozzarella cheese.

Preheat oven to 400°. Place the oysters in a large baking dish and bake for 10 minutes or until the cheese is brown and bubbly.

Sweet Potato-New Potato Feta Terrine

Serves 4

The contrasting colors of the layers make this deceptively simple dish look so elegant.

4   large new potatoes
2   large sweet potatoes
¾   cup feta cheese, crumbled
¾   cup broth or milk
    Salt and pepper

Peel and slice the potatoes. Place in a saucepan with enough water to cover. Bring just to boiling, and remove from heat and drain.

Preheat oven to 350°. Coat the bottom and sides of an oven-proof baking dish with a little olive oil. Place alternate layers of sweet potato, white potato, and feta, adding a little broth or milk with each layer. Bake for 40 minutes.

Serve directly from the baking dish, or cut in wedges or rounds with a cookie cutter.

Vegetable Couscous

Serves 6

1 ½ cups couscous
⅓   cup cooked black beans (see page 11)
¼   cup finely chopped shallot
2   tablespoons chopped sun-dried tomatoes
¼   cup finely chopped celery
¼   cup each finely chopped red and yellow pepper
¼   cup zucchini
⅓   cup chopped dried apricots
⅓   cup chopped fresh parsley
2 ½ cups vegetable or chicken broth
    Salt and pepper

In a large bowl, toss the couscous together with all ingredients except the broth and salt and pepper.

In a small saucepan, bring the vegetable or chicken broth to a boil. Pour the broth over the couscous and vegetables, and stir evenly to combine. Cover and let stand until the liquid is absorbed, about 10 minutes. Season with salt and pepper to taste. Serve warm or at room temperature.

Pecan, Oat, and Granola Encrusted Chicken

Serves 4

4	boneless skinless chicken breast halves
½	cups each plain granola cereal, rolled oats, and pecans
1	whole egg (or 2 egg whites)
2	tablespoons flour
1	tablespoon Dijon mustard
½	cup milk
1	cup black currants
⅓	cup black currant jelly (grape jelly may be substituted)
½	cup cassis liqueur

Combine the granola, oatmeal, and pecans in the bowl of a food processor and process to form a coarse meal.

Combine egg, flour, mustard, and milk to form a batter. Dip chicken breasts in batter, and lightly coat with the crushed granola-oatmeal-pecan mix. Arrange on a baking sheet and bake at 350° until golden brown and crispy, about 25–30 minutes (do not turn).

In a small saucepan combine the currants with the jelly and the cassis. Warm the mixture over low heat, stirring just until jelly is melted. (Note: If using canned currants, simmer for about 5 minutes or so, until liquid is reduced by half.)

To serve, ladle a pool of the sauce in the center of each plate and place a chicken breast on the sauce. Garnish each chicken breast with a bit of the sauce and top with a small dollop of sour cream.

Potato and Red Pepper Pancakes

Serves 4

2   medium Idaho baking potatoes, peeled and shredded
3   shallots, peeled and minced
1   large egg, beaten
1   red pepper, roasted, seeded, peeled, and chopped
2   heaping tablespoons chopped scallions
1   tablespoon crumbled feta cheese
2   tablespoons vegetable oil
     Salt and pepper to taste

Preheat oven to 375°.

Combine all ingredients. Heat the oil in a skillet over medium heat. Drop the mixture in by spoonfuls to form 8 small pancakes about ¼-inch thick. Cook about 8 minutes per side, until golden. Place on a baking sheet and bake in the oven for another 8 minutes.

Grilled Pesto-Tuna Steaks

Serves 4

4   6-ounce tuna steaks
½   cup pesto
¼   cup olive oil
1   cup chardonnay
¾   cup dry vermouth
     Juice of two lemons
½   tablespoon Dijon mustard
½   teaspoon Tabasco sauce

Combine the last seven ingredients for the marinade. Brush the tuna steaks well on both sides with the marinade. Grill over hot coals 6–7 minutes on each side or just until fish is opaque and flakes easily. Do not overcook. Serve with the Black Bean and Tomato Wild Rice featured on page 88.

Roasted Red Pepper and Squash Soup

Serves 4

⅓   cup dried cranberries

½   cup chardonnay

2   medium-sized squash (any variety of squash will do)

4   cups water or chicken or vegetable broth

4   red peppers, roasted, peeled, and seeded (see page 52)

1 ½   teaspoons chili-garlic paste*

¼   teaspoon nutmeg

⅛   teaspoon curry

2   teaspoons salt

½   cup crumbled gorgonzola cheese

Soak the dried cranberries in the chardonnay for 30 minutes or so; drain, reserving the wine.

Meanwhile, peel the squash, scoop out the seeds, and dice in about ½-inch pieces (should yield about 3 cups). Place in a saucepan and cover with the water or broth and bring to boil. Reduce heat to simmer and cook until squash is tender. Drain, reserving the broth.

Place the squash and red peppers in the bowl of a food processor and purée. Return the puréed mix to the broth and blend well. Add the chili-garlic paste, nutmeg, curry, salt, and reserved chardonnay. Heat just to the boiling point and remove from heat.

Ladle the soup into bowls and sprinkle with the cranberries and crumbled gorgonzola.

Available at specialty and Oriental food stores.

Scallops Étuvée with Confit of Leeks on Tabbouleh

Serves 4

½   medium-sized leek
1 ½ cups water or vegetable broth
16   bay scallops
¼   cup (½ stick) butter or margarine
2   tablespoons rice vinegar*
2   tablespoons orange juice
¼   cup chardonnay
1   teaspoon coriander
1   tablespoon chopped fresh cilantro
1   teaspoon paprika
1   teaspoon lemon pepper
½   teaspoon salt
1   cup prepared tabbouleh*

Clean and chop the leek (see page 27). Place the leek in a saucepan with the water or broth and bring to a simmer. Cook, tightly covered, for 20 minutes. Drain the leek, reserving the liquid. Return the liquid to the pot and boil until it is reduced to ⅓.

Sauté the scallops in the butter for about 8–10 minutes, until they are opaque. Add the reduced liquid from the leeks and simmer one more minute. Add the rice vinegar, orange juice, and chardonnay. Continue to simmer one more minute. Add the coriander, paprika, cilantro, lemon pepper, salt, and leeks. Remove from heat.

Mound the tabbouleh on serving plates and top with the scallops and leeks. Drizzle the liquid over the top and around the sides and serve.

Rice vinegar can be found in the Chinese food section of the supermarket. Tabbouleh, a finely cracked grain, can be found in the ethnic foods section. Prepare according to package directions.

Raspberry Swirl Cheesecake

2   cups sliced almonds

2   cups sifted all-purpose flour

1 ½ cups (3 sticks) butter or margarine, melted

1   cup lightly packed brown sugar

2   teaspoons almond extract

1   egg yolk

2   pounds cream cheese, softened

¾   cup mascarpone cheese, at room temperature

1 ¾ cups granulated sugar

2   eggs

¼   cup raspberry jam

¼   cup fresh raspberries

Grease the bottom and sides of a 9-inch springform pan.

Spread the almonds on a baking sheet and toast in a 375° oven for 5 minutes. Let cool and place in the bowl of a food processor and pulse just until the almonds are ground to a consistency of fine bread crumbs. Add the flour and pulse just until well combined.

In a mixing bowl, blend the butter and brown sugar. Add the egg yolk and almond extract. Gradually add the almond and flour mixture, stirring just until it forms a smooth mass. Spread the mixture evenly on the bottom of the springform pan.

With a mixture, beat the cream cheese, mascarpone cheese, and sugar together until light and creamy. Add the eggs one at a time, beating well after each addition. Spread the batter evenly over the crust in the springform pan. Combine the jam and raspberries drop by spoonfuls onto the cheesecake batter and swirl into the batter with a knife.

Reduce the oven heat to 325°. Set the springform pan into a larger baking pan and add hot water to about half-way up the sides of the springform pan. Bake for 1 hour or until the cheesecake is set. Remove the cheesecake from the oven and the water bath. Gently loosen the edges of the cheesecake with a knife to prevent the top from cracking. Let cool and refrigerate until serving.

Pan-roasted Rosemary and Mustard Pork Cutlets

Serves 4

4   boneless pork cutlets
2   cloves garlic, minced
½   cup plus 1 tablespoon olive oil
2   tablespoons maple syrup
4   sprigs fresh rosemary, chopped
¼   cup coarse-grain Dijon mustard
     Salt and pepper

Combine the garlic, ½ cup of olive oil, maple syrup, mustard, and rosemary in a large, shallow dish. Marinate the cutlets in the mixture in the refrigerator for at least 1 hour, turning occasionally. (This may be done a day ahead.)

Preheat oven to 375°. Remove the cutlets from the marinade (reserve the marinade for basting) and season with salt and pepper to taste. Heat 1 tablespoon of olive oil in an oven-proof skillet over high heat. Add the cutlets and sauté 6 minutes each side. Baste with the marinade, place in the oven and roast for 15 minutes. Serve with Spicy Onion Marmalade (next page).

Spicy Onion Marmalade

This is also delicious with other cuts of meat, such as New York strip steak.

Serves 4

1	tablespoon butter
3	cloves garlic, minced
2	pints pearl onions, peeled
2	medium red onions, halved and thinly sliced
4	tablespoons molasses
2	tablespoons red wine vinegar
3	tablespoons Tabasco sauce
¼	cup Worcestshire sauce
4	tablespoons coarse-grained Dijon mustard
1	teaspoon crushed red pepper
2	teaspoons cayenne
¼	cup brown sugar
	Salt

Melt the butter in a saucepan over medium-high heat. Add the garlic, pearl onions, and red onions. Sauté, stirring, until nicely browned and caramelized.

Add the red wine vinegar and cook, stirring constantly, for 2 minutes. Add the molasses, Tabasco, Worcestershire, and Dijon mustard. Continue cooking, stirring constantly, until liquid is reduced to about half the volume and thickened. Stir in the crushed red pepper, cayenne, brown sugar, and salt to taste and serve.

December's

mixed emotions steal like the shadow of the sundial across the face of another year. We are thankful for the opportunity to paint the four seasons from the palette of our pantry. We are sorry for the year we must surrender soon like the orchard's last apple to the gravity of time. The Inn, contented in its rug of Christmas color, dozes like a dreaming dog in the flicker of its own firelight.

We build a giant gingerbread house in the lobby. This endeavor is messy, labor-intensive, and costly. But any qualms are dispelled when we see a child wandering wide-eyed through the gingerbread door and shyly retrieving a piece of candy from the royal icing wall, under the watchful encouragement of a parent or older sibling.

The building of the gingerbread house has become for me each year's last loving ritual. Like dessert at the end of a good candlelit dinner, it seals the year with the satisfying resin of sweetness, the glow of rich color and soft light.

Roasted Turkey with Apple-Cranberry-Currant Chutney

2	tablespoons butter
6	unpeeled Granny Smith (or other good baking) apples, cored and thinly sliced
3	cups cranberries
1	cup currants
6	tablespoons calvados, applejack, or apple cider
½	cup brown sugar
4	teaspoons five-spice seasoning
1	teaspoon nutmeg
2	teaspoons cinnamon
1	10–12-pound turkey
3	tablespoons vegetable oil
2 ½	tablespoons coarse kosher salt
2 ½	teaspoons black pepper

Melt the butter over medium-high heat and add the apples, cooking just until apples are softened, about 8 minutes. Add the cranberries and currants and cook another 5 minutes, or until cranberries are softened. Add the calvados, applejack, or cider, and the brown sugar. Reduce the heat to medium and continue cooking until the mixture thickens. Stir in the spices and remove from heat.

Position the oven rack so the turkey will be just above the center of the oven and preheat oven to 450°. Remove giblets and neck from cavities of the turkey (reserve for later use, if desired). Rinse the turkey inside and out, and pat dry. Rub the outside with the vegetable oil and the salt and pepper. Loosely tie the legs with kitchen twine (optional).

Place turkey in a roasting pan and place in the oven with the legs pointed toward the back of the oven (this facilitates the basting process). Roast for 30 minutes, baste, and reduce the heat to 375°. Allowing about 12 minutes-per-pound cooking time, continue roasting, basting about every 30 minutes. If the breast meat seems to be cooking too fast, baste the breast section with a little ice water before each basting to slow the cooking process. Test the turkey for doneness by piercing the thigh. If the juices run clear, the bird is done.

Apple, Brie, and Spinach Turnovers

These make wonderful snacks or hors d'oeuvres.

Serves 4–6

1	cup all-purpose flour
6	tablespoons (¾ stick) butter, chilled and cut into small pieces
1 ½	tablespoons cold water
1	cup fresh torn spinach leaves (not packed down)
1	tablespoon olive oil
2	cloves garlic, minced
1	teaspoon nutmeg
	Salt and pepper to taste
1	medium-size apple (any good baking apple)
1	small wheel of Brie
2	tablespoons chopped sweetened dried cranberries

Using a pastry blender or fingers, gently incorporate the butter into the flour until it resembles coarse meal. Add just enough of the cold water for the dough to hold together. Shape gently into a ball, wrap in plastic, and chill for at least 45 minutes. (Dough can be made a day ahead.)

Slightly flatten the dough and roll it to about ⅛ inch thick. Using a cookie or biscuit cutter, cut into 2-inch circles.

Sauté the spinach in the olive oil for 5 minutes. Add the garlic, nutmeg, and salt and pepper to taste. Thinly slice the apple and cut the Brie into grape-sized pieces.

Preheat oven to 350°. For each turnover, arrange some of the spinach, dried cranberries, one apple slice, and one piece of Brie on each dough circle. Fold over and crimp the sides to seal. Bake for about 10 minutes, or until crisp and golden. (Brushing with a little milk or cream will enhance the appearance of the crust.)

Chicken, Spinach, and Tomatoes en Croûte

Serves 4

4	5-ounce boneless, skinless chicken breasts
1	frozen puff pastry sheet, thawed
1	cup washed and torn spinach leaves (not packed)
2	whole tomatoes, sliced
2	tablespoons chopped sun-dried tomatoes
¾	cup sliced mushroom caps
½	cup chopped scallions
4	slices mozzarella cheese (or ½ cup shredded)
½	cup shredded jack cheese
½	cup crumbled gorgonzola cheese
¼	cup melted butter or margarine

Grill or bake the chicken breasts for 20 minutes or until done. Cut each breast in 5 or 6 pieces.

Preheat oven to 350°. Roll the puff pastry out to form an 8 x 12-inch rectangle. Arrange the chicken pieces lengthwise down the center.

Layer on the spinach and sliced and dried tomatoes. Add the cheeses and sprinkle with the scallions and mushrooms.

Fold the dough over the filling, just enough to create a quarter-inch overlap. Dampen the edge of the dough with water and press slightly to seal. Place seam-side down on a baking sheet and brush with the melted butter. Bake 20 minutes or until golden. Slice and serve.

Shrimp and Sweetbreads à la Crystal Room

I created this dish at the Marott Hotel's Crystal Room. It always brings to mind the great people with whom I worked.

Serves 4

6	ounces veal sweetbreads
½	cup (1 stick) unsalted butter or margarine
1	tablespoon olive oil
12	medium-sized shrimp, peeled and chopped
¾	cup fresh mushrooms, chopped
2	medium tomatoes, peeled and chopped
½	tablespoon minced garlic
2	tablespoons lemon juice
⅔	cup chardonnay
2	tablespoon capers
	Fresh chives

Poach the sweetbreads in water for 20 minutes. Drain and clean off the filmy connective tissue. Slice the sweetbreads ¼ to ½ inch thick and blot on a clean towel , pressing gently to remove excess moisture.

Preheat a heavy skillet over high heat until very hot. Add the butter and oil and when it sizzles add the mushrooms, half the chopped tomatoes, garlic, sweetbreads, and shrimp and sauté on one side for 3 minutes. Turn the sweetbreads and shrimp and add half of the lemon juice and chardonnay. Sauté for 2 more minutes, and add the rest of the lemon juice and chardonnay. Continue to cook over high heat until the liquid in the pan forms a sheen over the shrimp and sweetbreads, about 5 minutes. Add the the capers and the remainder of the tomatoes.

Drizzle some of the pan juices on 4 serving plates. Arrange the sweetbreads in the middle of the plates with the shrimp around them. Top with the mushroom and tomato mix, and garnish each serving with two strands of chives.

Note: This recipe involves fairly sophisticated speed reduction and glazing techniques. If you are a beginning cook you might want to check into a video utilizing these techniques at your local library, or be prepared to hone your skills by trying the recipe more than once.

Sherry Roasted Duck with Kiwi and Cranberry Coulis

Serves 4

2   ducks
2   teaspoons garlic
1   teaspoon soy sauce
    Salt and pepper
¾   cup dry sherry
3   kiwis
1   tablespoon honey
½   cup cranberry juice

Preheat oven to 375°. Rinse the ducks thoroughly inside and out and pat dry. Rub the ducks with the garlic, soy sauce, and salt and pepper to taste. Place on a rack in roasting pan and roast for 30 minutes. Baste the ducks with half the sherry and roast for another 10 minutes or until done. (Test for doneness by piercing the thigh. The juices will run clear when done.)

While the ducks are roasting, peel the kiwis and purée in blender or food processor. Add the honey, cranberry juice, and the remaining sherry. Glaze the roasted ducks lightly with the sauce and serve the remainder on the sides.

Oyster and Crab Stuffed Artichokes

This looks very elegant, but is quite easy to prepare.

Serves 4

8   canned artichoke bottoms, drained
8   oysters, shucked
½   cup crab meat
½   cup crumbled Gorgonzola cheese
4   tablespoons grated Parmesan cheese

Preheat oven to 375°. Place one oyster in each artichoke bottom. Top with the crab meat and cheeses and bake for 10 minutes or until cheeses melt and turn golden.

Sautéed Fennel with Roasted Chestnuts and Bacon

A good winter dish to go with beef, lamb, or spit- or oven-roasted fowl.

Serves 4

1	dozen chestnuts, roasted
½	medium onion, sliced
2	slices bacon, diced
1	teaspoon molasses
2	fennel bulbs, sliced

Preheat oven to 350°. With a sharp paring knife, make a cross-cut incision in the top of each chestnut. Bake for 8 minutes. Allow to cool enough to handle and peel.

Sauté the onion and the bacon over medium heat until the onion turns brown. Add the fennel and continue to sauté for 5 minutes. Add the molasses and continue to sauté until everything turns a light carmel color.

Add the chestnuts to the onion and fennel mix and serve.

Spiced Almond Tart

Makes a 9-inch tart

1 ⅔	cups cake flour
1 ½	cups granulated sugar
¼	cup brown sugar
¾	cup (1 ½ sticks) butter, melted and cooled slightly
2	eggs, beaten
2	tablespoons almond extract
1	teaspoon anise
1	teaspoon ground cloves

Preheat oven to 350°.
Lightly oil a 9-inch tart pan with vegetable oil and dust lightly with flour.
Combine flour and granulated and brown sugars in a bowl. With an electric

mixer set on low speed, add the melted butter, eggs, almond extract, anise, and cloves. Beat until smooth. Spread batter evenly into the prepared tart pan. Bake for 30 minutes or until the top is brown.

Cherry Pecan Bread

Makes 3 loaves

1 ½   cups maraschino cherries, well drained
6   cups all-purpose flour
2 ¼   teaspoons baking soda
½   teaspoon salt
1   cup instant vanilla pudding mix
2 ¾   cups sugar
3   eggs
1   tablespoon vanilla
2 ½   cups buttermilk
½   cup vegetable oil
1   cup coarsely chopped pecans

Grease and flour three 8 x 4-inch loaf pans. Preheat oven to 350°.

Coarsely chop the maraschino cherries and set aside.

Sift the flour, baking soda, salt, and pudding mix together in a large mixing bowl. In another bowl beat the sugar, eggs, and vanilla together with a mixer. Add the dry ingredients and the buttermilk and oil alternately to the sugar and egg mixture, stirring just enough to blend. Do not overmix.

Toss the chopped pecans in enough flour to lightly coat them. Fold the pecans and chopped cherries into the batter. Scoop the batter into the prepared loaf pans and bake for 35–40 minutes or until done. Remove from oven and allow to cool in the pans on a wire rack for 15 minutes. Remove the loaves from the pans and finish cooling on a wire rack.

Glossary

Al dente: an Italian term meaning "firm to the bite," used most frequently in reference to pasta and vegetables.

Arrowroot: a thickening starch.

Arugula: a leafy, lettuce-like vegetable, excellent for garnishes.

Coulis: strained concentrated juice and pulp.

Couscous: a type of very quick-cooking North African and Middle Eastern pasta, made of steamed semolina pellets.

De-glaze: to add just enough liquid such as wine or broth to pan drippings produced in the sautéing or pan roasting of a food item, usually meat, to create a richly flavored liquid or sauce. Since the idea is to attain intensity of flavor we almost always add just enough liquid to lift the residue from the pan when the drippings and juices are still hot.

Ganache: a thick, rich filling ideal for truffles and tarts.

Hummus: a chickpea paste often flavored with garlic, paprika, and lemon

Jicama: a South American vegetable which tastes somewhat like a cross between an apple and a potato.

Julienne: to cut in fine strips approximately ⅛ inch thick by 2 inches long.

Kalamata olive: a highly flavored dark purple colored olive.

Pine nut: the edible seed of many different species of pine.

Ramekin: a circular, oven-proof, earthenware baking dish of varying sizes.

Sweetbread: the thymus or pancreas of a young calf, used for food.

Taboulleh: a finely cracked wheat popular in Middle Eastern dishes.

Tapenade: a Spanish-type sauce.

Terrine dish: a rectangular dish with removable sides.

Tomatillo: a small member of the tomato family.

Vinaigrette: a mixture of vinegar and oil.

Wasabi: a Japanese root similar to horseradish.

Sources for Ingredients

Earthly Delights
Hope, MI

For edible flowers, wild mushrooms, herbs, and specialty fresh produce.

1-800-367-4709

J. B. Prince
New York, NY

For hard-to-find cooking utensils.

1-212-683-3553

Midwest Imports
Chicago, IL

*For a wide variety of ingredients used in the preparation of several of the pastries
and desserts in this book. To request a catalogue, call*

1-800-621-3372

Index

Irish Brown Soda Bread, 25
Lemon Poppy Seed Bread, 55
Zucchini Nut Loaf, 75

SAUCES, SALSAS, AND CHUTNEYS

Apple-Cranberry-Currant Chutney, with
Roasted Turkey, 123
Blackberry Hollandaise, with Salmon
Poached in Lettuce, 19
Black Currant Sauce, with Lamb and
Dublin Coddle, 29
Black Currant Vinaigrette, with Grilled
Salmon Salad, 64
Blood Orange Vinaigrette, 79
Cantaloupe Avocado Salsa, 79
Champagne and Vanilla Yogurt Sauce,
105
Chef Vernon's Roasted Red Pepper
Remoulade, 105
Corn and Black Bean Relish, with Red
Snapper Rings, 84
Green Peppermint Sauce, with Irish
Whiskey Truffles, 33
Kiwi and Cranberry Coulis, with Sherry
Roasted Duck, 127
Mango, Pepper, and Black Bean Salsa,
with Pecan Encrusted Amberjack, 53
Onion Steak Sauce, 11
Papaya Avocado Salsa, with Pan-fried
Trout, 48
Peach Chutney, with Pan-roasted Pork
Chops, 86
Spicy Onion Marmalade, 121
Tomato, Eggplant, and Caper Salsa, 56
Warm Tomato and Herb Vinaigrette, with
Cornish Hens, 104

SOUPS AND SALADS

Artichoke and Mixed Green Salad, 46
Buttermilk Pike Potato Salad, 73
Corn, Cucumber, and Potato Chowder, 85
New Potato and Artichoke Salad, 52
Pan-roasted Eggplant and Garlic Soup, 93

Purée of Scallop and Red Pepper Bisque,
56
Red Bean, Corn, and Red Pepper Chow-
der, 95
Roasted Eggplant and Pepper-Scallion
Salad, 37
Roasted Red Pepper and Squash Soup,
117
Walden Inn Black Bean Soup, 10
Walden Inn Power Salad, 43
Warm Spinach Salad with Mandarin
Oranges, 22
Wild Rice and Turnip Greens Soup, 38

TART(S) (*Non-dessert*)

Goat Cheese Tart, 101
Indiana Sweet Corn and Red Pepper Tart,
94
Zucchini and Chive Tartlets, 87
Zucchini, Dried Tomato, Spinach, and
Gorgonzola Pie, 70

VEGETABLES AND SIDE DISHES

Colcannon, with Atlantic Salmon
Galway Bay, 26
Corn and Red Pepper Pancakes, 111
Dublin Coddle, with Lamb and Black
Currant Sauce, 28
Fennel and Bacon Patties, 6
Gorgonzola and Roasted Vegetable
Terrine, 108
Peppers, Roasted, 52
Potato and Red Pepper Pancake, 116
Sautéed Fennel with Roasted Chestnuts
and Bacon, 128
Sweet Potato-New Potato Feta Terrine,
114
Vegetable Broth, 97
Vegetable Couscous, 114
Wasabi and Cheddar Potato Cakes, 35